THE TECHNIQUE OF TORCHON LACE

The Technique of
Torchon Lace

Pamela Nottingham

B.T. Batsford Ltd   London

ISBN 0 7134 0268 7

Filmset in 'Monophoto' Apollo by
Servis Filmsetting Ltd, Manchester
Printed and bound in Great Britain by
Anchor Brendon Ltd, Tiptree, Essex
for the publishers B. T. Batsford Ltd
4 Fitzhardinge Street, London W1H 0AH

Contents

Contents

Introduction

Torchon lace has always been known as Beggars' Lace, a derisory term as its designs cannot be compared with the beautiful laces of the seventeenth and eighteenth centuries. It was made and sold by European peasants, but was not introduced into England until the second half of the nineteenth century. As the making of lace by machine was perfected the bobbin lacemakers were unable to compete economically, and they endeavoured to find lace that was quicker and easier to make. In the middle of the nineteenth century the Maltese style was adopted, as the leaves, plaits and picots were worked more quickly than the traditional point ground lace. Torchon was simple to make, as the geometric designs could be readily understood, and since few stitches were required it became increasingly popular.

Today Torchon is regarded by many people as an inferior hand-made lace, the main reason being perhaps that it can be imitated by machine. Indeed it is true that machine made Torchon lace may be identified by a mistake – perhaps a missing twist – appearing at regular intervals, whereas the hand-made lace has the irregularities which arise only when bobbins are moved by hand on the pillow.

However, Torchon lace does have an established place in bobbin lacemaking today. It is better than its machine-made counterpart, as the pattern can be planned and worked individually to suit the purpose for which it is intended. It can be made exactly to size, with corners, to edge a handkerchief or item of table linen. Threads can be selected to match the fabric, and if a good quality linen is used it will launder well and last indefinitely. The prickings are straightforward and can be prepared to any size. Confidence and interest will increase with ability, and in a fairly short time one can plan patterns, create designs and work a lace that is original. It is a joy to make and, for many people, it is a pleasure to work a lace that is easily seen and understood.

Lacemaking is a challenge, and the intricacies of Bucks Point lace and the complex trails of old Beds-Maltese are very demanding; Torchon on the other hand can provide relaxation. It can also be made into useful gifts, items for sales of work and narrow edgings, since a small article can be made in only a few hours. For those who demonstrate the craft, Torchon on the pillow is clear, definite and – to a layman – probably more comprehensible and interesting than a more complicated lace. Through teaching the craft I know the many problems which lacemakers are likely to encounter, and in this book I have tried to include the necessary useful information and patterns in a clear and logical manner.

I wish to thank Patricia Philpott for taking the photographs and Jean Miller for checking the information. Once again I express my gratitude to my husband, Arthur Johnson, for his encouragement and help, and above all for his infinite patience and skill in producing all the diagrams which make this book possible.

1 – Equipment and Preparation

THE LACE PILLOW

There is considerable variety in the shape of pillow used for lacemaking today, often very different from the traditional type used when lace was a cottage industry in the villages of Bedfordshire, Buckinghamshire and Northamptonshire. Large square and round pillows, well able to accommodate large patterns and many bobbins, were supported on stands – known as maids – but these are seldom seen today.

A small, flat pillow has attractions for the inexperienced worker; it is easy to make, light to carry, requires no support and allows the bobbins to be spread out for quick recognition. However, after the initial stages are complete, the flat

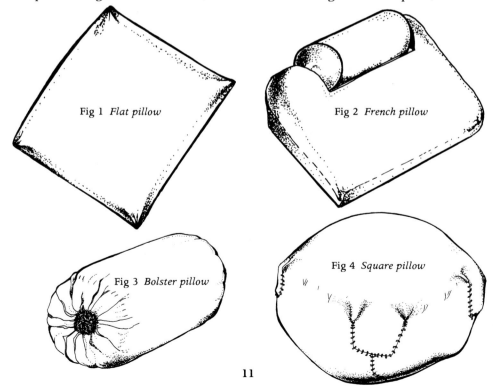

Fig 1 *Flat pillow*

Fig 2 *French pillow*

Fig 3 *Bolster pillow*

Fig 4 *Square pillow*

pillow becomes irksome, the lace has to be moved frequently – a difficult and time consuming occupation – and there is inadequate working space in which to control a large number of bobbins. Too often the card will rise from the pillow or the threads will ride up the pins.

The shape of the traditional pillows allows the weight of the bobbins to keep the threads taut, and the lace may be made continuously round the pillow. The bobbins fall to the front, back and sides over a large area, so that they are found easily when needed; consequently, large pieces of lace, wide edgings, collars, fans and mats can be undertaken. Yet the lacemaker of today may well discard the round bolster pillow without analysing why she finds it difficult to manage, or without attempting to solve the problems. The fact that many thousands of these pillows were in use when people made lace as a means of livelihood suggests that, if used correctly, they must still be worth considering. The pillow must be large, with a diameter of at least 300mm (12in); indeed, the bigger the diameter the better the pillow – many old ones measured 500mm (20in). Thus the working area at the top of the pillow is flat and the curve is gradual. The length rarely exceeds 450mm (18in).

It is important to position the pillow in a stand for comfortable working. There were several styles; the folding type (see figure 8) is particularly useful as it can be adjusted for different pillows, and it may also be packed flat for storage. When using the bolster on a stand it is pulled towards the lacemaker so that her knees are underneath and the bobbins are close enough for ease of handling; it is essential that she sits high enough to look down to the top of the pillow.

Alternatively, the pillow can be placed on a box with semicircles cut from

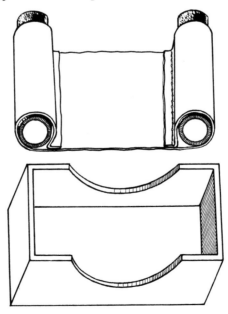

Fig 5 *Temporary stands for bolster pillows*

opposite sides, or a temporary support can be made using a piece of fabric 400mm (16in) wide and 500mm (20in) long (figure 5). Hems 100mm (4in) deep are made at either end and cardboard tubes or rolls of newspaper inserted. The length of fabric depends on the size of the pillow but, if adjusted to suit a particular pillow, it can be very useful.

The disadvantage of these methods is the problem of finding a comfortable working position. The normal table is too high, and a lower table prevents the lacemaker from sitting close to the work. It is possible and very comfortable to sit on an upright chair, place the bolster on the knees and allow it to rest against the back of a second chair (with the seat away from the worker) or against a table. It is essential to experiment until a convenient position is found.

The French pillow is very suitable for narrow edgings, and a pillow of this type was on sale in Bedford at the beginning of the century as a Torchon pillow.

To make a flat pillow

To make a flat pillow suitable for stitch practice and for small mats and motifs, refer to figures 1 and 6. Take a piece of plywoood 350mm (14in) by 400mm (16in)

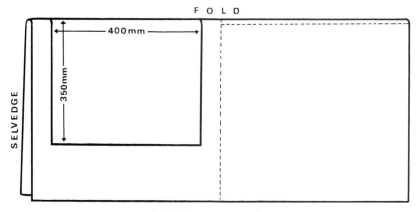

Fig 6 *Making a flat pillow*

and remove the sharp corners with sandpaper. Use dark green or blue drill – or other strong cotton fabric – to make a bag the same size as the board, leaving one end open. Slide the board inside and stuff one side only with finely chopped straw or hay. The straw must be forced in tightly to achieve a hard pillow. Oversew the remaining side. After several months of use it may be necessary to re-open the pillow and add more straw to maintain a really hard pillow. When working, raise the end of the pillow to slope it towards the lacemaker. The remaining fabric will make two rectangular cover cloths to match the pillow.

To make a bolster pillow

Refer to figures 3 and 7. A piece of strong canvas or hessian 950mm by 700mm (37in by 28in) is folded in half so that the 700mm (28in) edges are together. Sew

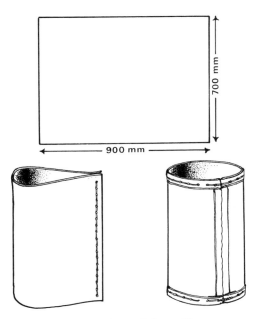

Fig 7 *Making a bolster pillow*

firmly 25mm (1in) from the edge to make a cylinder. Turn in and sew 30mm (1¼in) hems at each end, leaving a gap to insert the tape. Turn through so that the raw seam edges are inside, and put a tape through one hem and pull up tightly. Put the bolster case on a firm surface, place a piece of fabric inside across the hole and stuff the bolster with chopped straw. Some people like to insert a disc of strong card to help achieve the shape, but this is not essential. The straw must be in small pieces to achieve a good, even shape, and it must be hammered well down using a wooden block and a mallet. When sufficient straw has been forced inside, run a tape through the other hem and draw up tightly. Before tightening the tape a piece of fabric, and, if desired, another disc of card, may be inserted. A second cover is made, usually in green or blue, and this may be removed for laundering. Extra rectangles of hemmed fabric will be required to dress the pillow.

To make a pillow stand

Refer to figure 8. Using a saw and plane, shape two blocks of wood, each 450 × 80 × 25mm (18 × 3 × 1in), to form two curved bars on which to rest the pillow at the top of the stand. Drill holes in the undersides of the bars to take the legs. Using 50 × 25mm (2 × 1in) wood, construct two legs 775mm (31in) long, and two legs 700mm (28in) long; join together one of each length (on either side of the stand) with a nut and bolt (to allow the stand to be folded away after use), and attach the bars to the tops of the legs as shown. Struts placed at the front and back will strengthen the construction, and the two lengths of cord (maintaining the distance apart of the legs) should be adjusted until the bars at the top are in the correct position to hold the pillow. The back bar is higher than the front to hold the pillow firmly when the pillow is turned as the lace is made.

Fig 8 *Making a pillow stand*

BOBBINS

Bobbins are probably among the most interesting tools of any craft, examples of the everyday articles of one age becoming the prized antiques of another. The requirements of the bobbin are threefold: it must hold thread, be easy to handle and have sufficient weight to keep the thread taut. Only in England has the craftsman, with skill and ingenuity, fashioned local wood – plum, cherry, apple, rosewood – adorned it with brass wire, pewter bands or spots and added beads for weight to make the finely decorated bobbins which give so much pleasure to those who use them. Bobbins made of bone have coloured lines and dots as decoration, and those with inscriptions and names were either given as love tokens, or kept to commemorate family occasions or to record happenings of

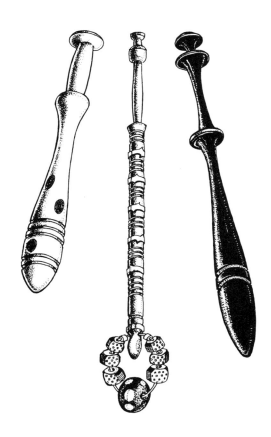

Fig 9 *Bobbins: South Bucks, East Midland (typically English), French*

local interest; now they arouse curiosity and give insight into village life of over a century ago. Today, with the increasing interest in the craft, bobbins are being made once more and so another old skill, that of the bobbinmaker, has been revived.

Of little interest to the collector are the small wooden bobbins turned on pole lathes by the chair bodgers in the Chiltern Hills. Short and thick, their weight lies in the thickness of the wood, and without beads they are quick to use, but they need the fall of the bolster pillow. In Belgium and France the bobbins are usually larger, with slim necks to hold a lot of thread and a bulbous body for easy handling. It is essential to select bobbins of the same type and similar weight, and to keep the thread between lace and bobbin short so that the bobbins do not fall away over the edges of the pillow. The pillow should be moved frequently so that the pins are placed in the pricking at least 30mm (1¼in) behind the top of the curve. If the lace is worked to the front of the flat area, the bobbins fall forward and become muddled and the threads become twisted and tangled.

Long hat pins may be used to hold the bobbins to one side when not in use. Placed 25–50mm (1–2in) from the sides of the pricking and level with the working position, they prevent the bobbins from falling too far back. If these pins are slid under a number of bobbins, with the point of the pin pushed into the pillow and the pin pulled up to a vertical position, a small bundle of bobbins will be supported by the pin. When the bobbins are required the pin may be dropped down carefully and they will fall back into use in the correct order.

THE THREAD

Care must be taken to select a thread suitable for the lace to be made. When the pattern has been chosen it is transferred onto squared paper in order to produce the pricking. The thickness of thread depends on the grid; recommendations are given only as a general guide, and it may be necessary to wind bobbins and try out an unknown thread. Many lacemakers make a sample piece of lace before beginning the actual work. The thickness of two threads may appear the same, but a three-cord thread will work up more closely than a two-cord thread, as it is more highly twisted.

When the skill of the lacemaker is evaluated and the time taken to make the lace considered, linen thread will be the first choice for most work. It is strong and hardwearing, and the finished lace could one day become a family heirloom. Cotton threads are obtained more easily, they are less expensive, and the lace is pleasing; however, it lacks the crisp appearance of linen. Silk threads are used infrequently as they are difficult to obtain, and practice is necessary to get good results; but they do make attractive trimmings for dresses and blouses. When using man-made fibres it is essential to work a sample piece of lace. Some threads are very resilient, and it becomes difficult or even impossible to achieve the good tension and clear lines which give lace character.

The pattern features also require consideration. A pattern with many cloth shapes, and cloth stitch and twist ground, may need a finer thread than a similar pattern interpreted with half stitch. A thread which shrinks when laundered is to be avoided but, if it is used, a coarse pricking is recommended; otherwise washing will make the ground close and the cloth dense.

The fabric on which lace is to be mounted should match or contrast in colour and be of similar weight to the threads selected for the lace. When a project is planned, all materials should be purchased before the work is undertaken. Lace to be mounted under glass may look more attractive using finer threads which show the intricacy of the weaving, as there is no problem of laundering.

Wise choice of the gimp thread (see page 39) may enhance a pattern; a soft shiny thread with the minimum of twist used to outline distinctive pattern features will strengthen the design. The gimp thread must be thick enough to be seen as an important contribution to the pattern.

A wide variety of threads in many thicknesses is available for traditional white and ecru lace. If a particular coloured thread is required it may be necessary to find a suitable thread and adapt the pattern. To match the thread and pattern it is quite usual to try out a thread on a range of grids; fortunately Torchon lace is very easily transferred onto graph paper, and a pricking can be made to the required size.

Most of the patterns in this book were made on a 2.5mm ($\frac{1}{10}$ in) grid and worked in DMC Fils à Dentelles no. 70, and when necessary a no. 5 Pearl cotton was used as a gimp thread. The collar on page 140 was worked in no. 8 Pearl cotton and the collar on page 110 was worked in DMC Retors d'Alsace no. 40.

No. 5 Pearl cotton is suitable for most Torchon patterns unless a fine thread, such as Retors D'Alsace nos. 40, 50 or 60, is used, when no. 8 Pearl cotton is preferable.

Below are suggested threads suitable for the grids given at the back of this book.

Grids A   1mm ($\frac{1}{24}$ in) Useful for identification purposes. It can be placed alongside the pricking or lace footside to work out the distance between the holes or stitches. Too fine for normal use, but could be worked with Retors D'Alsace no. 60

B   1.5mm ($\frac{1}{16}$ in) Retors D'Alsace no. 40 or 50

C   2mm ($\frac{1}{12}$ in) Brilliante D'Alsace no. 20 or Retors D'Alsace no. 30 DMC Cordonnet no. 150, Swedish linen thread nos. 80 or 90

D   2.5mm ($\frac{1}{10}$ in) Fils à Dentelles no. 70, Swedish linen no. 50

E   3mm ($\frac{1}{8}$in) Swedish linen no. 35

F   5mm ($\frac{1}{5}$in) For working out patterns to be reduced later

J   Retors D'Alsace no. 40

K   Threads as for C or D

L   Threads as for J

M   Threads as for J

With the exception of the Swedish linen all the threads mentioned are cotton, and are manufactured by Dollfus-Mieg & Cie. Fils à Dentelles, intended for tatting, is produced in one thickness only. Cordonnet, intended for crochet, is available in a wide range of thicknesses, but the finest (no. 150) is the only thread suitable for bobbin lace. Pearl cotton may be obtained as nos. 5, 8 or 12. Brilliante D'Alsace and Retors D'Alsace are similar threads used for machine embroidery; the former has a whiter appearance. These come in a range from no. 20 (Brilliante only), 30, 40, 50 and 60. As with all threads, the higher the number the finer the thread.

An increasing number of different threads are being offered for bobbin lace, usually on large spools. When the lacemaker is skilled in the craft it will be possible to try these threads and choose those which are most pleasing and which give a good finished result.

PATTERNS AND PRICKINGS

Pattern selection

The choice of lace pattern for a particular purpose is important and needs careful consideration. A piece of lace to be seen at a distance requires a bold design composed of large definite areas using suitable stitches, such as cloth stitch or closely-worked half stitch. Any spiders (see page 50) should be large and enclosed by firm surroundings. A mass of rose ground is pleasing but indefinite. Ground (see page 101) should recede to emphasise the prominent features, and when tallies (see page 71) are used they may be grouped for effect. Contrast is all important. Lace may be enhanced by the choice of fabric on which it is mounted; mid blue or deep red, for example, beneath white or unbleached threads, is very attractive. Lace behind glass, in pictures, trays, finger plates on doors or under paperweights has added interest and is protected.

All lace must have a decisive pattern, but when it is to be seen within the immediate environment it may be worked using a finer thread and a wider variety of stitches. Half-stitch shapes, a half-stitch ground with an interesting arrangement of tallies, leaves used as flower motifs and the many interesting varieties of rose ground may be appreciated when seen in detail in front of a pleasant background. Lampshades made of panels of mounted lace allow the lace to be silhouetted against the diffused light, accentuating the delicacy of the work. Wise use of thick gimp threads and definite forms contrasting with the lightness of a well chosen ground will show the skill of the lacemaker.

Initially it will be necessary for the inexperienced worker to take a pricking and copy the lace samples in this book. Later it will be possible for the pricking to be given a personal interpretation, using the shapes and pinholes given, but with an individual choice of stitches. In time, the lacemaker will begin to create original patterns; the possibilities are endless and enjoyment will grow as lace is made to the exact shape and size required. Torchon lace is geometric in design and the planning of new patterns is comparatively easy. The making of the lace is straightforward and regular, it is achieved quickly, and will give tremendous satisfaction as work of pleasing originality is created.

To plot the pattern on graph paper

For neat and accurate lace and for ease of understanding when working, the pattern must be exact, the holes well spaced and the rows of holes must be straight. New designs may be planned and lace can be copied by the proficient lacemaker, but to gain experience it is advisable to copy the arrangement of dots for prickings given in this book, and then to copy existing prickings. It is necessary to understand how lace is worked before attempting to transfer the pattern to squared paper. (A selection of grids is given at the back of this book.)

Always use a sharp pencil and mark errors with a small ring around the incorrect dot; the use of an eraser rarely obliterates the dot completely and may cause confusion.

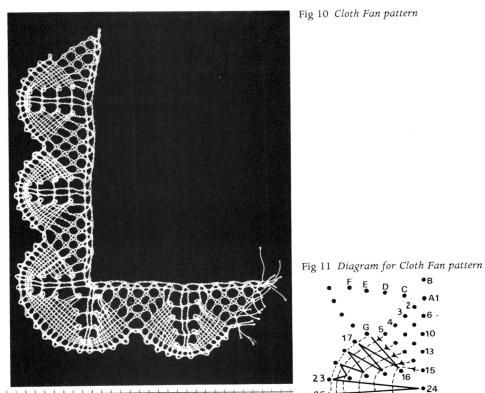

Fig 10 *Cloth Fan pattern*

Fig 11 *Diagram for Cloth Fan pattern*

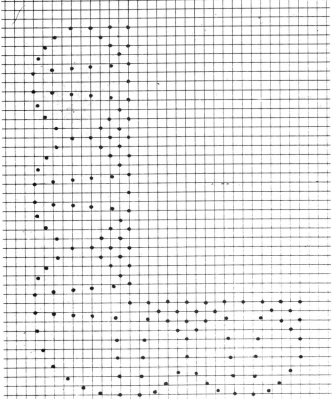

Fig 12 *Pricking for Cloth Fan pattern*

Use the graph paper with lines running vertically and horizontally. To mark the footside place dots at alternate intersections on a vertical line.

Lace is worked diagonally and it is essential to develop a logical method when plotting the pattern. An excellent plan is to build up the pricking in the way in which the lace is worked. Mark in the longest row of diagonal row of holes and then add any pattern features.

For an example refer to figures 10, 11 and 12. Mark in the diagonal row of holes from A1—four, excluding the foot which has already been positioned – and complete the triangle of ground. Note the footpin independent of each triangle, and mark in several triangles. Mark in pinhole G to the left of the point of the triangle; this sets the position for the curve of head pins. Sketch in the curve using a stencil or pair of compasses. Note position of holes 23 and 25, which are at the highest point of the curve and equidistant from 24 on the footside. Place a straight edge between 15 and 23 to establish a line on which lie the inner holes of the fan, and position them according to the pattern or lace. Mark in the other pinholes on the curve and, as a check on accuracy, draw in the path of the weaver. Mark in a number of repeats to achieve an accurate pattern.

It is usual to plan the entire piece of work before pricking so that correct lengths are made. This will be explained further when corners are discussed. When the pricking is made, two pieces are necessary; they can be used in turn so that the entire length or four corners are not pricked. It is important that the join should occur where it affects the lace least; along a diagonal line between holes is most convenient. In the simple pattern explained above, a join can be made along a horizontal line just below G, 5 and 10.

To make the pricking

A pin vice fitted with a no. 8 Sharps sewing needle, a piece of thick cork or polystyrene, drawing pins and special thick glazed pricking card are required. Prickings must be made on a flat surface, and the pricker held in a vertical position to avoid distortion. The fine needle is used so that the holes are small and the pins remain rigid to support the threads and achieve good tension. Fine, clear lines in permanent black ink on the pricking are the lacemaker's instructions. Inaccurate marking will cause frustration and wasted time, and the colour from an ill-chosen pen or crayon may rub off onto the lace.

To use the patterns in the book

To assist the lacemaker the first patterns are shown on grids. Soon the lacemaker will use the photographs as a guide. However the working diagrams are all based on a 2.5mm ($\frac{1}{10}$ in) grid, and tracings may be taken for the purpose of making a pricking. As this is a rather inaccurate method it is not recommended. The pattern should be worked out on graph paper. To facilitate this, a grid may be prepared on clear acetate sheet, and lines 2.5mm ($\frac{1}{10}$ in) apart should be scratched onto the sheet with a sharp point. When laid over the working diagram the position of the holes will show through the grid.

2 – Basic Stitches and Techniques

PREPARING THE EQUIPMENT

Preparing the bobbins

Wind six pairs of bobbins with DMC Fils à Dentelles no. 70 thread. A knot is never found in lace; the thread between the bobbins must be free of knots. Hold a bobbin in the left hand and the thread in the right. Wind over and away in a clockwise direction (see figure 13). Wind evenly as much thread as possible onto this bobbin. Cut the thread. Take a second bobbin in the left hand and wind half the thread from the first bobbin back onto the second bobbin. Although so much winding may seem tedious, thread becomes tangled and twisted if a length is left unwound. Make a hitch on each bobbin (see figure 14). Allow about 200mm (8in) of thread between the bobbins. Until all the required pairs are ready, wind the

Fig 13 *Winding thread onto the bobbin*

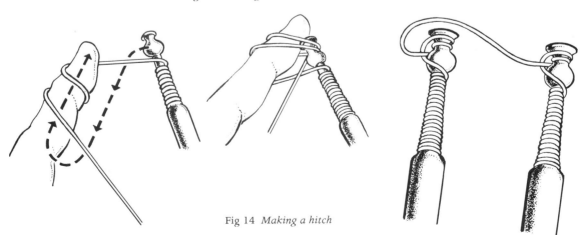

Fig 14 *Making a hitch*

22

200mm (8in) of thread around one bobbin of the pair and leave the pair beside the pillow. If the pairs of bobbins are to be moved, put them in groups of four pairs and secure each with a rubber band, as much time can be wasted untangling pairs.

Making the pricking
This is made using 2.5mm ($\frac{1}{10}$ in) graph paper as shown in figure 15. Extend each section for at least 150mm (6in).

Preparing the pillow
Make holes with the pin vice very close to the four corners of the pricking. Pin the pricking firmly onto the pillow using lace pins. It is unnecessary to put extra pins along the sides of the pricking, the thread will get caught and is easily broken. Allow 60mm ($2\frac{1}{2}$in) of card to show, and cover the lower part of the pricking with a cover cloth. If the edge of the cloth is folded under it will be found that the fold lies closely upon the pillow and is preferable to the hem or selvedge. Keep it in position with one pin at either end.

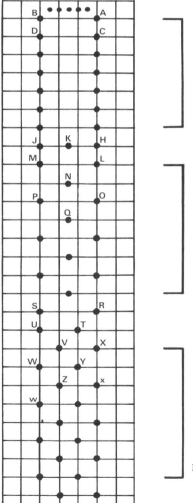

Fig 15 *Making the pricking*

THE BASIC STITCHES

The names given to stitches vary from one locality to the next, and sometimes the same name can mean different stitches. For example, reference is made to plaits in chapter 9, and these are a form of continuous half stitch. In some areas these are known as 'legs' and in those areas the leaves which are made by weaving one thread about the other three are known as plaits. Fortunately photographs can clarify this kind of misunderstanding.

The following three stitches (see figures 16 and 17) are sufficient for almost all the patterns in this book. Practise them until they can be worked with some speed.

Half stitch	ab
Cloth stitch or whole stitch	abc
Cloth stitch and twist	abcb

Put pins in the five holes at the top of the pricking and hang one pair of bobbins round each. Hang the other pair on a pin at A. This pair is the weaver and temporarily the bobbins may be marked to facilitate understanding the early stages.

Cloth stitch

Using the two right-hand pairs, ie the pair from A and the pair to the left of it, count the threads from left to right as 1, 2, 3, 4. This refers to position and not to the bobbin so that it is necessary to count before each move. Using the left hand, move 2 over 3. Using both hands, move 4 over 3 and 2 over 1. Using the left hand, move 2 over 3.

The weaver pair from A has passed to the left through the straight or passive pair. Discard the passive pair to the right hand side of the pillow. Use the weaver and the next pair to the left of it, make a cloth stitch and discard the passive right hand pair. Use the weaver and the next pair to the left to make a cloth stitch, repeat twice more and the weaver will be on the left hand side.

Move the right-hand thread of the weaver pair over the left-hand thread, repeat this move. This will be referred to as twisting the weaver twice. Note that the right hand thread always passes over the left regardless of the position of the pair. Lift the weaver pair, raising the necks of the bobbins so that the pinhole can be seen.

Put a pin in B inclining it outwards to the right of the weaver pair. The weaver pair is held in position by the pin and stitches will be worked to return it to the left-hand side of the work. Take the left-hand pair (weaver) and adjoining pair and work a cloth stitch. Discard the left-hand pair to the left of the pillow. Continue across the work to C. When the weaver is on the right-hand side, lift the penultimate pair, and put the pin in C to the left of the weaver pair. Continue until the hands move quickly and the stitch is worked without difficulty.

To achieve good tension, hold the weaver firmly at the end of each row, and after putting up the pin, 'stroke' the passive bobbins to pull the threads taut.

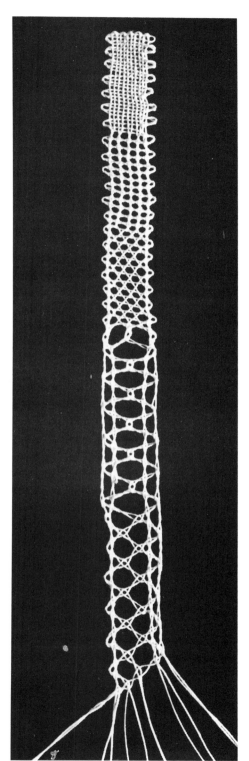

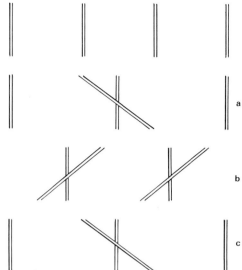

Fig 17 *Movement of bobbins to make stitches*

Fig 16 *Basic strip: cloth stitch, cloth stitch and twist, half stitch, footside and ground*

Cloth stitch and twist

Refer to illustration 17; work moves a, b, c, and then repeat move b. Notice that the passive pairs lie on the pillow with one twist on each; care must be taken to retain that twist when bobbins are moved. Extra care should be taken to maintain good tension. This stitch is rarely used in the form practised, but this is an excellent way to learn it. It is used at the ends of rows of cloth stitch, sometimes for ground, and always for the edge or footside.

Half stitch

At the end of the row, when the pin is in position, work cloth stitch and twist to cover the pin. Discard the pair as usual and use the next pair with the weaver to work half stitch; refer to illustration 17 and work a, b, only. Discard a pair as usual and bring in the next pair for the next stitch. Continue, but note that only one thread is travelling across the work and the pairs lie twisted on the pillow. At the end of the row work the last stitch as cloth stitch and twist. Put up the pin and return. It is important to work cloth stitch and twist before and after the pin to achieve a firm edge which will withstand wear and laundering.

BEGINNER'S BRAID

This is an attractive way of learning the footside – the straight edge onto which the fabric is sewn – and involves using one stitch only: cloth stitch and twist.

To prepare for the braid, which will require the six pairs of bobbins, work holes H and J. Take the centre pairs and work cloth stitch and twist, put up pin K between the pairs and work another cloth stitch and twist to cover the pin.

To work the footside on the right

Using three pairs of bobbins, take the third pair from the right and work cloth stitch and twist (abcb) twice to the right through two pairs (ie the third pair works cloth stitch and twist through the adjacent pair and on through the outer pair), so that this pair is now at the edge. Put up a pin at L to the left of *two* pairs. (In future this will be referred to as putting the pin inside two pairs.) Twist the outer pair once more and ignore it. Use the other pairs to work cloth stitch and twist to cover pin L.

To work the footside on the left

Take the third pair from the left-hand edge, and work cloth stitch and twist twice towards the left. Put the pin M inside two pairs (ie to the right of two pairs), ignore the outer pair and use the other two pairs to cover the pin. Again use cloth stitch and twist.

To make the pattern

Take the two centre pairs and work cloth stitch and twist, put up pin N between the pairs and cover with cloth stitch and twist. Continue; work O as L, P as M and Q as N. A complete understanding of the stitches and footside is essential before learning to work the ground.

The footside and ground

The net, which is known as the ground, links the footside with the more definite and interesting pattern areas. Ground may be worked in a variety of ways but the simplest and most usual way is using half stitch. To begin, arrange the bobbins as follows. Complete pins R and S. With the centre pairs work a half stitch and put up pin T between the pairs; cover the pin with a half stitch. With the left-hand pairs work cloth stitch and twist, put up pin U between the pairs and cover with cloth stitch and twist. The right-hand pair from U and the left-hand pair from T work half stitch; pin V is put up and covered with half stitch. The left-hand pair from V and the pair from U work cloth stitch and twist; pin W is put up, an extra twist is given to the left-hand pair, and pin W is covered with cloth stitch and twist.

Lace is usually made in England with the footside on the right. The normal sequence for working footside and ground is as follows. Take the third pair from the footside edge, work cloth stitch and twist twice (the weaver is at the edge), put up pin X inside two pairs, ignore the outer pair and cover the pin. Now discard the right-hand pair, and use the left-hand pair and the right-hand pair from V to work half stitch, pin Y, and cover with half stitch. A ground pin is worked half stitch, pin, half stitch. Now use the left-hand pair from Y and the right-hand pair from W to work pin Z. The edge is worked with the left-hand pair from Z and the pair from W with cloth stitch and twist, pin w, cloth stitch and twist. To continue work pin x, remember to use the third pair from the edge and to work from x diagonally across the pattern.

LACE TERMS

Lace instructions may be expressed in many ways, lacemakers use different terms and the written work may be interpreted in several ways. Fortunately photographs and illustrations help to overcome the problem. To avoid confusion, an explanation of some of the terms used is given below.

To cover the pin

When a pin is in position it is covered by working a stitch using the same pairs of bobbins. It is usual to use the same stitch before and after the pin. It is also sometimes referred to as enclosing the pin.

The weaver

This is the pair which travels through the other pairs in cloth or half stitch. It is frequently known as the worker or leader.

To hang pairs on a pin

The pairs are arranged so that they fall one inside the next. Thus the outside threads are the same pair but adjacent threads belong to different pairs. This method is used when beginning the footside or when pairs are introduced at a plait crossing.

To hang pairs on a pin in order

This is used at the beginning of a piece of work when pairs will lie side by side. It is also used when pairs are brought in one at each pinhole, for example when beginning with a diamond shape. The pairs are placed on the pin so that the threads from each pair remain side by side. Care must be taken to check that a weaver is not hanging along with other pairs as it will be impossible to ease the loop away later.

CUTTING OFF THE BOBBINS

When threads have been cut off a piece of work, they may be re-used; it is not necessary to rewind for each pattern. To avoid handling the thread, cut the bobbins from the lace, using a blunt pair of scissors, and working as in figure 18. Hold the pair of bobbins in the left hand and the pair of scissors in the usual way in the right hand. Keep the blades closed and take the thread over and under as in

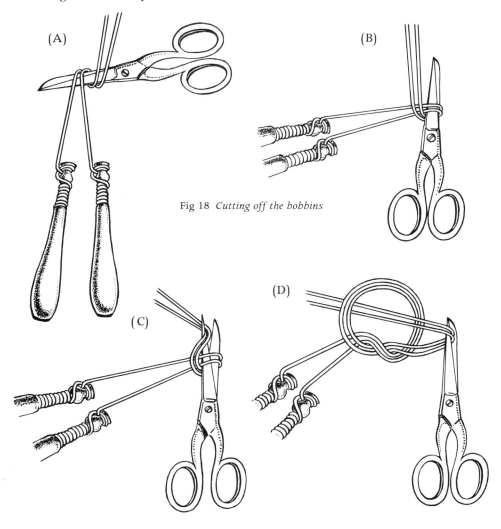

Fig 18 *Cutting off the bobbins*

figure 18A. Move the pair of scissors through a 90° angle until parallel with the threads and to the right of them as shown in figure 18B, then open the blades and trap the threads above without cutting them, as in figure 18C. Pull the blades down through the loop, and at the same time raise the threads and bobbins in the left hand up to help the loop over the points of the blades, as in figure 18D. Cut and allow one bobbin to fall from the hand to tighten the knot automatically. Practice and patience are necessary to master this, but it is a quick and efficient method, and worth the time taken to achieve it. Remove the hitch from one bobbin of the pair, wind the thread, including the knot onto this bobbin for a yard or two and then replace the hitch.

ADDING A NEW THREAD

When the knot appears when making the lace, proceed as follows. Introduce another bobbin, fasten it to a pin and place the pin in the pillow to the side of or behind the pricking. Allow the thread to fall alongside the thread with the knot, and temporarily fasten the bobbins together with a rubber band or wire twist. Use the double thread for about 25mm (1in), depending on the distance apart of the stitches. Then discard the bobbin with the knotted thread and continue with the new thread. The discarded bobbin may of course be introduced to replace another thread after the knot has been cut off.

3 – Narrow Edgings and Circular Motifs

CLOTH FAN PATTERN

Refer to figures 10 and 11, and prepare the pricking from figure 12, on page 20. Hang two pairs of bobbins on pin A1, one pair on each of pins, B, C, D, E and F, and two pairs on pin G. Using the two pairs hanging from A1, twist the right-hand two bobbins three times. Work cloth stitch and twist to cover the pin. Give one extra twist to the right-hand pair and discard. Take the left-hand pair from A1 and the pair from B, work cloth stitch and twist but do not put up a pin. Discard the right-hand pair – this is the twisted passive pair.

To work the ground

Take the other pair and the pair from C to work a half stitch, put up pin 2 and cover with half stitch. Discard the right-hand pair and continue to work diagonally using the pair from D to work a half stitch. Put up pin 3 and cover with half stitch. Continue to work pins 4 and 5 using pairs from E and F. Ground pins are always covered in Torchon lace and it is usual to work the same stitch before and after the pin. The most common stitch used is half stitch but cloth and twist is used to give a firm strong lace. Remove the support pins C, D, E and F, and pull the threads into position carefully. It is advisable to remove pin B later as it supports a passive pair of threads.

To work the footside

Take the third pair from the outside edge (the right-hand side) and work cloth stitch and twist with the next pair to the right; continue, and work another cloth stitch and twist with the outside pair. Twist the outside pair once more and put up pin 6 inside (to the left of) both pairs. Ignore the outer pair and work cloth stitch and twist to cover the pin.

This sequence of stitches is used normally on the footside in Torchon lace. The additional twist on the outside pair strengthens the edge – if the thread is fine more twists may be added. Occasionally variations occur and two twisted pairs may be introduced as passives; sometimes two or more passive pairs are used untwisted. Work the three remaining ground pins in the diagonal row. Continue until pin 15 has been covered. Remove pin B.

To work the fan

There are several ways of working a Torchon fan with this arrangement of holes. The use of cloth stitch is not frequently seen but it is straightforward to do; it gives a firm edge and is easily laundered. Other methods are shown on pages 136, 138 and 141.

Using the pairs on G, twist the two right-hand bobbins three times and cover the pin with cloth stitch and twist. With the right-hand pair as weaver, work to the right through the next five pairs in cloth stitch. Put up pin 16 to the left of the weaver and work back through the same five pairs in cloth stitch. Twist the weaver once and work cloth stitch and twist with the outside pair. Put up pin 17 and cover with cloth stitch and twist. Continue weaving as shown in figure 11, working through one pair less each time when weaving to the right. When weaving to the right from pin 23, work the cloth stitch and twist edge as usual, work through the next two pairs in cloth stitch and then twist the weaver three or four times to fill the space. Twist the pair from the fan once and work cloth stitch and twist with the weaver. No pin is used for this stitch. Continue, giving the weaver additional twists, to work through the next two pairs similarly. After the pair from pin 16 has been worked the weaver, which is now third pair from the outside edge, works the normal footside and pin 24. The weaver travels back to pin 25, and the fan is completed, re-introducing the pairs as required.

One repeat pattern is complete. Many patterns can be worked in definite sections, and this speeds the work and is clearer to understand. In this pattern, work the ground, half of the fan, the foot pin and the second half of the fan.

To work the corner

Figures 10 and 11 clarify the method used to work the corner. Corner pin X has to be used twice; when needed a second time the pin is taken out and replaced after the stitch has been made.

SIMPLE EDGINGS

Friends and relations are fascinated by the lacemaker's pillow, and sooner or later everyone wants to produce a quantity of lace quickly and without too much effort. These patterns may be used with a variety of threads to trim lingerie, baby gowns and blouses, handkerchiefs and table linen, or adapted as trimmings for various small articles. The four introductory patterns have been selected for this purpose; each pattern shows a different arrangement of threads on the headside, two in cloth stitch and two in half stitch. These may be useful to incorporate when designing patterns later. It is possible to work out a corner for almost any Torchon pattern provided that a few simple rules are followed.

To plan the corner

Refer to figure 19. Take an unframed mirror with a straight edge and hold it vertically on the line across the pricking. Keep it at the same angle, ie 45° from the footside, and move it down the pricking until an attractive corner is seen. Refer to figure 20, the Spanish Torchon pattern, and use the mirror to see the effect on the

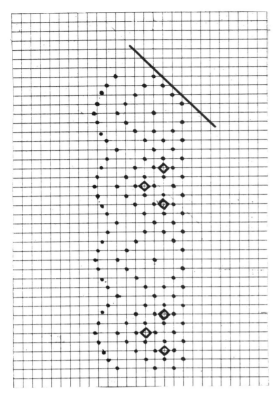

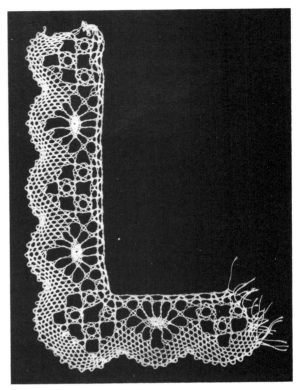

Fig 19 *Planning the pattern*   Fig 20 *Spanish Torchon pattern*

lace. With experience the lacemaker will be able to 'see' the effect using the pricking only when lace is not available. Similarly the practised lacemaker will be able to decide if the corner selected may be worked easily. The following points should be considered.

(1) The corner diagonal line lies between rows of holes. A good corner never has a row of holes actually on the diagonal line. A footside corner pinhole is put in position on the line, also one additional pinhole on the headside.

(2) No solid pattern feature can extend over the diagonal. When making the lace, every hole above the diagonal corner line is worked, the corner pin is covered and the pillow is turned to begin the next side. The pattern must be complete on either side. Problems may be overcome by planning two narrow shapes with twisted pairs travelling across the corner. (See figure 165.)

(3) Spiders cannot be placed centrally in a corner unless irregularities are introduced. Normally the pattern will be arranged with spiders on either side of the diagonal. (See figure 66.)

(4) A continuous trail within the pattern is broken on the diagonal. It will be worked as the end of a diamond until two pairs remain at the final pinhole. When the pillow has been turned another trail is begun again from a point. (See figure 25.) This also applies to a narrow trail; if a continuous effect is

required a half stitch is made with the appropriate pairs across the corner line. See figure 167 – the inner trail has been worked with the additional half stitch, but it has been omitted in the outer trail.

(5) If the pattern is asymmetric, the pattern must be reversed at the centre of the side. (See figure 111.)

(6) Patterns may require some adjustment to achieve an attractive headside. A continuous trail has more pinholes on the outside edge, and the inner pinholes are used more than once at the discretion of the lacemaker. (See figure 20.) The addition of one extra pinhole at the corner gives a neat result when two fans meet. (See figure 111.) A design which is severely flattened is unattractive; it is essential to carry the pattern out to 'fill' the corner at the outer edge.

To make the corner pricking

Refer to figure 21 and prick through two sheets of paper all the holes below the line. Cut one sheet of pricking on the diagonal line, ie just beyond the first pricked holes. Turn it over so that the rough side is uppermost. Place it in position on the other pricking, figure 22, to make the corner. Add the corner pinhole and make some adjustment on the outside edge. A pricking on card may be made from the paper copy. For absolute accuracy the complete pattern should be worked out on squared paper. It is useful to make the corner pricking with the same number of pattern repeats either side of the diagonal. The correct number of repeats can be pricked onto another piece of card for use between corners.

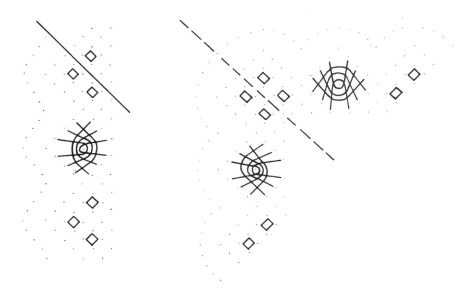

Fig 21 *Making the corner pricking*   Fig 22 *Placing it in position*

BEGINNING THE PATTERN

Where to begin

Any pattern which is joined to complete the work must be started in a position where the join will show as little as possible. For example, a half stitch trail at the edge of lace should be joined at the lowest point, where it will be noticed less than at the fullest part of the curve. (See figure 20.) Obviously fans and scallops must be worked in entirety (see figures 25 and 165). Within the pattern it is preferable to work solid cloth or half stitch at the beginning, as threads from a less stable or more open area may be sewn in less noticeably later. (See figures 111 and 145.)

In figure 164 the half stitch was worked before the fan. Apart from the advantages mentioned above, the lacemaker will benefit as the number of pairs available for the fan has been settled, and they are firmly anchored to help in achieving good shape and tension. Lace may be started along a straight line at right angles to the footside, or on one or more diagonal working lines. If a strip of lace is required it may be more useful to begin on a straight line.

How to begin neatly

Beginning along a straight line is explained on pages 59 and 70. The method used when lace is joined is described here. For personal pride and satisfaction a neat pillow is important. Untidy ends not only offend the eye but also prevent good results when attempting to assess the suitability of thread for the pricking, or of the pattern for a specific use.

Figures 20 and 23 are used to clarify the explanation. When the first feature to be worked has been decided, in this case A1, 2, 3, notice where the pairs would come from if these holes were in the next repeat pattern. As A1 is on the footside, two pairs will fall to the right of that pin. In order to anchor the pairs, place them round the pin and work a cloth stitch and twist. The outer (right-hand) pair is discarded, and the other pair works with the passive pair which is hung on pin B. This pin will be removed later when the passive is well established in the lace.

Pins 2 and 3 are worked as ground pins with 'legs' from the spider, therefore the two pairs may be hung in order on pin C – in order as they are used separately. Immediately these pins are covered, pin C is removed, and the threads eased down into position. As the left-hand pair from pin 3 will be taken into the half stitch trail at pin 4, a weaver is required on pin E. The remaining pairs must be in the trail and are hung in order on pin D.

To estimate the number of pairs needed in the trail, allow sufficient to fill the trail after pairs have been left out for the rose ground; this will vary according to the thickness of the thread and the closeness of the half stitch preferred. The pair from E weaves through the first pair from D in cloth stitch and twist, through the other pairs from D and one pair from pin 3 in half stitch. Pin 4 is put up to the left of the weaver pair, and the half stitch edge trail continued. Pin D is removed and the threads eased down, this gives a neat beginning to the work. It is necessary to work cloth stitch and twist before and after the edge stitch to achieve a firm edge.

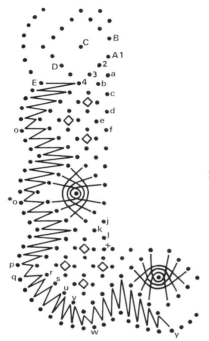

Fig 24 *Adding an extra pair to the corner headside*

Fig 23 *Beginning on the footside*

Order of working

(1) The trail is worked to pin o.

(2) In order to work the rose ground units, work pins a, b and c. Two units may be completed. Details for the rose ground stitches are given on page 60; figure 60(A) is used in this pattern.

(3) Now work pins d, e and f, in order to work the third unit.

(4) The trail is worked from o to *o.

(5) Three foot pins and three ground pins are worked in preparation for the spider.

(6) Work the spider using three 'legs' on each side. A sampler showing a variety of spiders is shown on page 63, figure 68 is similar to the spider worked here.

(7) Pins in the same position as pins 1, 2 and 3 are worked next.

(8) Work the trail to the top of the next curve.

The corner

To retain a neat close half stitch trail on the corner headside it is advisable to add an extra pair. At pin p refer to figure 24. When pin p is in position, take the extra pair and put one bobbin under the weaver pair, bring the loop up and allow the pair to fall inside and to the right of one thread of the trail. It will be hanging on the weaver threads; work to pin q. Pins j, k and l and two rose ground units are worked. Continue the trail to w, bringing in threads at r and s and leaving out threads after u and v. Notice that the inner holes of the trail are used more than once. Work pin x and turn the pillow. Work two more rose ground units; this releases pairs for the trail which can be worked to y. When pin w has been covered, the next pair is knotted and placed back across the work and cut off later.

SCALLOP AND DIAMOND PATTERN

This pattern has a firm edge and a quickly worked half stitch trail within the design. Refer to figures 25, 26 and 27.

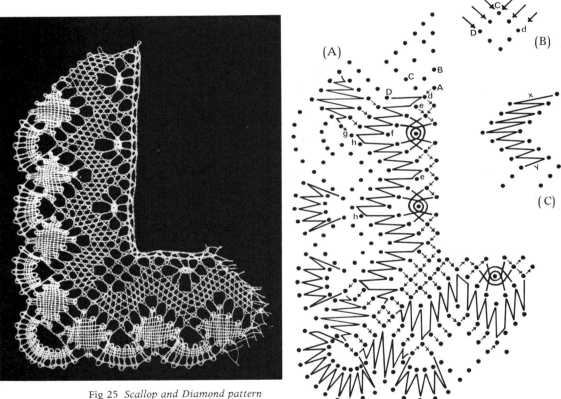

Fig 25 *Scallop and Diamond pattern*

Fig 26 *Diagram for Scallop and Diamond pattern*

To establish the number of pairs required

Perhaps it is convenient to wind all the pairs of bobbins in preparation, but generally speaking it is preferable to use pairs as required and avoid the anxiety of wondering how to include the stated number. To assess the number, count the pinholes on the longest diagonal, and include the points where pinholes would fall if the pricking was marked as ground. In figure 26A, count the pinholes from the left side point of the diamond through g, and D; count one extra between D and C and two extra between C and the footside (thirteen altogether). Add to this figure two pairs extra on the footside; one is necessary to work the straight edge and the other to provide the passive pair. It will be seen from the photograph that no additional pairs are needed for the scallop in this pattern. However, pairs are included in headside trails and fans at the discretion of the lacemaker.

To begin
Set in the three footside pairs by working pin A; the left-hand pair will be taken into the trail at d.

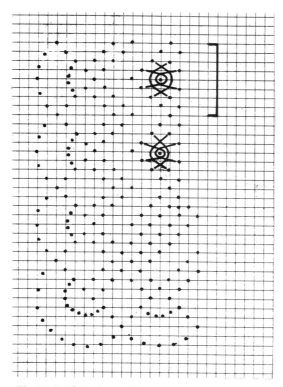

Fig 27 *Pricking for Scallop and Diamond pattern*

The trail
It is necessary to work out the number of pairs required between D and d. Pin D will support the trail weaver, and a pair from the footside will be taken in at d. A number of pairs to be included will be supported on pin C. Refer to figure 26B. Imagine Dd to be the widest part of a diamond; two pairs are required to begin at C, and one more pair at each pinhole. The arrows indicate pairs required. As D

and d are already accounted for, hang four pairs on C. The trail may be worked simply as in figure 26C, the weaver working from side to side in the same manner as the headside trail in the previous pattern. As the weaver travels unequal distances – compare x and y – the number of threads falling diagonally varies according to the direction of the trail. (See figures 84 and 145).

To overcome this unevenness the path of the weaver may be altered; refer to figure 26A. Work in half stitch from D to d in the usual way, cover pin d and discard the right-hand pair for the footside. The left-hand pair works in half stitch with the next pair to the left. Pin e is put up between these pairs and is covered. Discard the right-hand pair for a ground stitch. The left-hand pair is the weaver and works the trail as far as g. Pairs will be introduced from support pins on the left, and left out for the spider on the right. Pins g and h are worked similarly to pins d and e, but pairs are discarded to the left and the weaver moves to the right. This method looks well in half stitch but is unattractive in cloth stitch. When a cloth stitch trail is worked, pinhole f may be replaced by two holes positioned close together; to achieve an even head this method has been used in the motif shown in figure 34.

The spider
In order to have the two right-hand pairs available for the spider, two footside pins and one ground pin must be worked. The left-hand pairs come directly from the trail. Ensure that there are three twists on each 'leg' and work the spider. Immediately give each 'leg' three more twists, and work the two footside pins and one ground pin. This not only sets the spider in position but also provides the pairs necessary to work the trail. Work the trail from h to e. This releases pairs for the cloth diamond.

The diamond
Four pairs hang from the trail for the right-hand pinholes; hang four pairs on support pins for the left-hand pinholes. It is neater to give each pair a second twist when entering or leaving half stitch.

The scallop
The left-hand pair at the bottom point of the diamond becomes the weaver. Twist it twice, and work to the left through the next two pairs in cloth stitch. Twist the weaver twice, and work cloth stitch and twist with the outside pair. These four pairs work the scallop; complete it and leave the weaver on the right-hand side ready to begin the next diamond.

Order of working
One pattern repeat has been completed. When patterns are analysed and a definite order of work established, the lace is made more quickly and there is less likelihood of mistakes. This pattern illustrates this fact particularly well. The order of work is as follows: e to h, two footside and one ground pins, spider, two footside and one ground pins, h to e, diamond, scallop; continue.

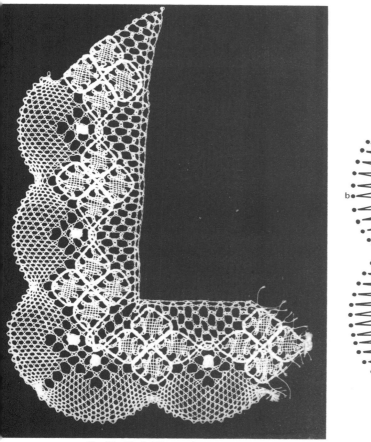

Fig 28 *Cloth Diamonds pattern*

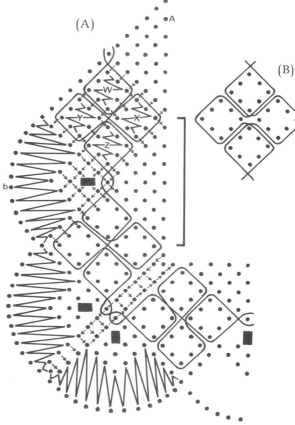

Fig 29 *Diagram for Cloth Diamonds pattern*

CLOTH DIAMONDS PATTERN

The heavy gimp threads which surround the cloth diamonds give character to this pattern. Refer to figures 28 and 29. To avoid weakness in the ground, cloth stitch and twist is used before and after the pin instead of the usual half stitch. Similarly weight is added by replacing one ground stitch with a tally.

Begin working at pin A and complete the footside pins and five rows of ground. Work one more footside pin, and six pairs hang ready for the cloth diamonds. Hang six pairs on support pins to the left of the diamonds.

Gimp thread

A gimp thread should be thick enough to emphasise the pattern and contrast with the other thread used. A soft thread which 'spreads' to give a definite outline is preferable to a highly twisted one. For example, pearl cotton is better than crochet cotton. Pairs of threads are always twisted twice before the gimp is passed through. When the gimp thread is taken to the right, it passes under the first and over the second thread of any pair. When it is taken to the left, it passes over the first and under the second thread of any pair. The pair is twisted twice to enclose the gimp thread. When gimp threads lie together it is unnecessary to twist between them; as far as possible they should lie flat alongside each other, unless a particular effect is desired.

Care must be taken to ensure that a shape is enclosed completely. Refer to figures 29A and 29B. The arrangement of threads in 29B will leave an ugly hole in the centre. Hang the gimp pair on a support pin behind the working area, bring six pairs through, twist them twice each and work the cloth diamond W. Bring both gimp threads to the bottom point of the diamond and cross them. Do not twist yet, but take the gimp round and through six pairs for diamond X. Now twist to enclose the gimp and work the diamond. The same gimp thread encloses the whole of diamond X and passes through six pairs for diamond Y. It encloses diamond Y, crosses the other gimp, each one passing through three pairs for diamond Z. It will be seen that the same thread has enclosed both X and Y.

To continue the pattern, work the next row of ground (ie footside and five ground pins).

The headside

As already described, it is important to have cloth stitch and twist before and after the pin on the outer edge of half stitch; work to pin b. The number of pairs in the half stitch is at the discretion of the lacemaker; in figure 28, in addition to the weaver, five pairs were hung on a support pin at the beginning. Using pairs from the half stitch edge and a pair from Z, complete the first row of half stitch, pin, half stitch ground. Work the second row, including the tally.

The tally

This is probably the most difficult stitch to do well. Practice is necessary; if possible consult a lacemaker as practical instruction makes the understanding far easier. Always twist each pair twice at the beginning and take the second thread from the left as the tally weaver. Pass it over the third thread and under the fourth. Refer to figure 30. The outside threads must be kept straight and taut to achieve a good shape, the centre thread may be ignored and the weaver must remain in the hand of the worker throughout. The weaver is responsible for an even tally and should be eased into position closely about the outside threads. When the required length has been worked the weaver is twisted with the right-hand pair, and the centre and left-hand pairs are also twisted together. The weaver must be supported to prevent loss of shape, and the pair without the weaver taken into use first.

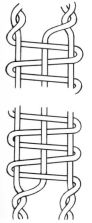

The single stitch enclosed by gimp

Pass the crossed gimp threads through the appropriate pairs, twist the pairs twice and work the ground stitch, put up the pin and cover with the same stitch. Give the pairs each an extra twist and bring the gimps back through, then cross them in preparation for the diamond. Work the remaining ground stitches below the tally and complete the half-stitch headside.

Fig 30 *Working the tally*

Order of working

Patterns are worked more quickly if a definite order is established. In this pattern, work as follows.

(1) Triangle of ground stitches
(2) Four diamonds with gimp
(3) The first half of the half-stitch head
(4) Two diagonal rows of ground near the headside including the tally
(5) One row of ground and the stitch surrounded by gimp
(6) The last row of ground near the headside
(7) Completion of the half-stitch head.

SMALL CIRCLES

The emphasis in the first four patterns has been simplicity and speed. This can be extended to include small motifs with a variety of uses, in fine thread they may be mounted under paperweights or, in coarser thread, several may be joined to make an edging or a complete mat. They can be used for insertion, either in a traditional manner for table linen or cushion covers, or in a variety of colours in blouses, nightgowns, aprons etc. This method is suitable only for small motifs as distortion will occur towards the edge of large motifs.

Designing small circles

Refer to figure 31. Mark in diagonal intersecting lines as shown. With the centre at the point of intersection, draw a circle of the size required, and mark the dots. Refer to figure 32 and indicate with dots the limits of each section and the main

Fig 31 *Designing a small circle*   Fig 32 *Marking the main pattern feature*

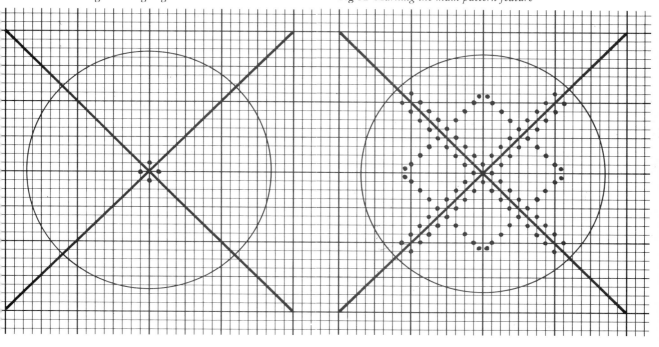

Fig 33 *Marking the path of the weaver*

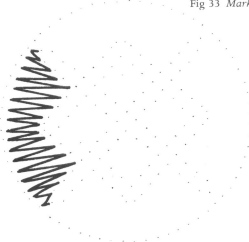

pattern feature. Refer to figure 33. Draw in the path of the weaver and space the holes evenly on the outside curve.

The following four samples show a variety of alternatives using the same pricking. Each is worked in four separate parts. Use the working diagram to complete one section, turn the pillow through 90° and work the next section. The method is the same as for the corner working on any edging. Complete the other sections.

Circle with cloth stitch and half stitch diamonds

Refer to figures 34 and 35. This is straightforward; five pairs are hung on a and the right-hand pair weaves to the left through the other four pairs. Cloth and twist is preferable on the outside edge. Arrows indicate the direction of threads, and the path of the weaver is also shown.

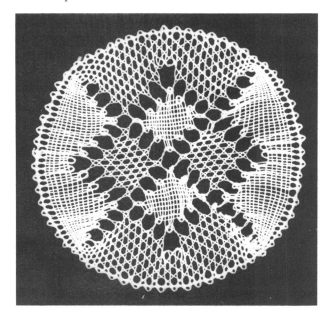

Fig 34 *Circle with cloth stitch and half stitch diamonds*

Fig 35 *Diagram for figure 34*

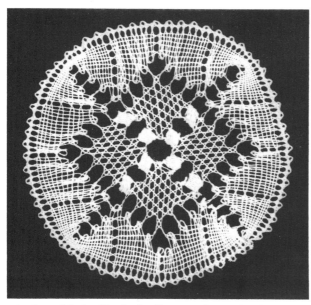

Fig 36 *Circle with half stitch diamonds and tallies*

Fig 37 *Diagram for figure 36*

Circle with half stitch diamonds and tallies

Refer to figures 36 and 37. The pattern is worked similarly to the above pattern but the straight pairs are twisted in the cloth edging for added interest; this also helps to keep good tension. The diamond will be worked as in the previous pattern, and then the tallies worked between sections as the pillow is turned. Finally tallies will be worked to complete the motif. Remember to sew in the pair without the tally weaver before the other pair.

Circle with spiders and tallies

Refer to figures 38 and 39. Again ignore the tallies until a complete section has been worked. The pair left out after pin b works half stitch, pin c, half stitch with

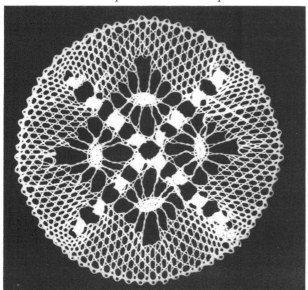

Fig 38 *Circle with spiders and tallies*

Fig 39 *Diagram for figure 38*

a pair from a support pin. Similarly pins d, e, and f are worked. When the spider has been made, the pair at f works diagonally through the spider 'legs' to enter the half stitch head at k.

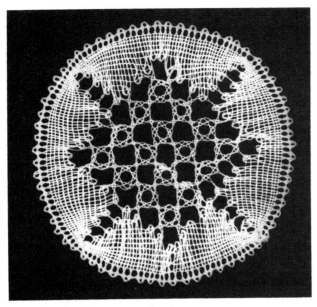

Fig 40 *Circle with rose ground centre*

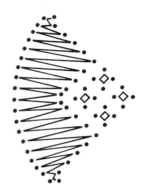

Fig 41 *Diagram for figure 40*

Circle with rose ground centre

Refer to figures 40 and 41. Rose ground always looks attractive, as the turning of the pillow and change of direction does not show in the finished lace.

4 – Square and Rectangular Mats

SQUARE MATS

The only factors which limit the size of these mats are the size of the lace pillow and the number of bobbins available. The principles of pattern making and the method of execution are the same for all sizes.

Planning and design
These are planned in the same way as the small circular motifs and consist of four corners about a central point. Figure 42 shows the method for planning the mat;

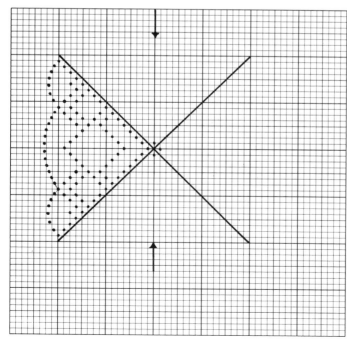

Fig 42 *Planning a square mat*

Fig 43 *Square mat with spiders and rose ground*

Fig 44 *Diagram for figure 43*

Fig 45 *Square mat with spiders and half stitch*

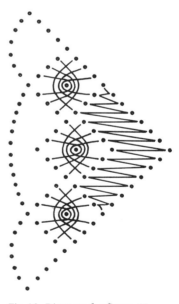

Fig 46 *Diagram for figure 45*

usually it is composed of four identical triangles. Well chosen pattern shapes and stitches create interesting and effective results. Study figures 43, 45, 47 and 49; the same basic pricking was used for all of them with only minor modifications. The use of half stitch on the edge makes the mats look larger and more round. Notice the three spiders: the small spider in figure 43 is bounded by ground

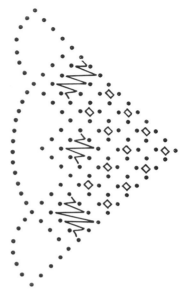

Fig 47 *Square mat with cloth stitch diamonds and rose ground*   Fig 48 *Diagram for figure 47*

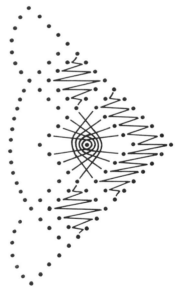

Fig 49 *Square mat with spiders and cloth stitch diamonds*   Fig 50 *Diagram for figure 49*

stitches and hardly noticeable, the spider in figure 45 is easily recognised, while the larger spider in figure 49 is definite and interesting. The use of rose ground in figure 47 gives a broad all-over pattern, and the division into triangles is obliterated. When designing a piece of lace, the purpose for which it is intended is very important; on the whole, bold designs in Torchon lace are the most striking.

Fig 51 *Pricking for figure 49*

Method of working

To facilitate the working, mark in the diagonal lines between the triangles on the pricking. In addition place an extra cover cloth along a line indicated by arrows in figure 42. This line indicates the position of the footside if an edging was being made, and the diagonal line of working from the footside remains clear. Each time a section is completed and the pillow turned, the cloth should be repositioned. As work progresses, the pins in the first section will be in the way of the bobbins. These pins must be pushed down into the pillow and a piece of clear acetate sheet laid over the heads; it will be kept in position if it is pushed under the cover cloths on either side. Refer to figures 43 and 44, 45 and 46, 47 and 48, 49 and 50 for the method of working. Figure 51 gives the pricking for 49.

RECTANGULAR MATS

Planning and design

Any size may be designed and worked, but it must be remembered that sufficient bobbins are required to work the full width at one time. In order to overcome this problem, the larger mats can be made in sections, although designed as one. An edging with footside and four corners can be worked, and a centre rectangle, using the same row of footside pins, can be worked independently. They can be joined after each section is complete by hand sewing.

Fig 52 *Pricking for figure 53*

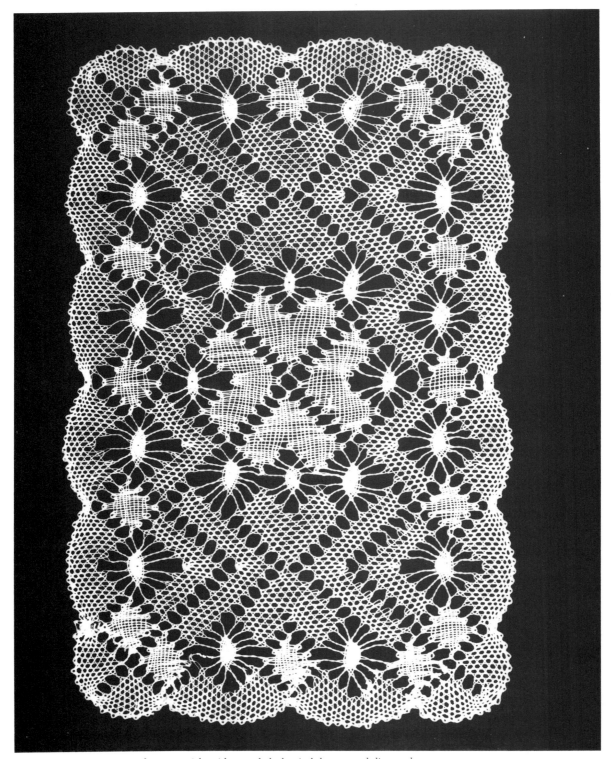

Fig 53 *Rectangular mat with spiders and cloth stitch hearts and diamonds*

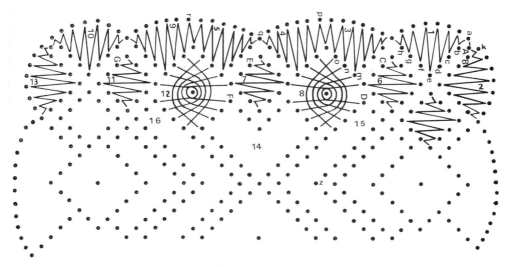

Fig 54 *Diagram for beginning the rectangular mat*

Method of working

Prepare the pricking according to figure 52. Refer to figures 53 and 54. Turn the illustration and the pillow so that the top edge is to the left. Place ten pairs round A; they must be placed one inside the next and *not* in order. Similarly place eight pairs round B. The right-hand two threads on A are the weaver threads for fan 1. Weave in half stitch to the left through the next three pairs and on through the next pair in cloth stitch and twist. Put up pin a to the right of the weaver. Ignore the remaining five pairs and pin them to one side out of the working area. Weave back to the right, through the first pair in cloth and twist and through the other three pairs in half stitch. Continue in half stitch through one more pair, (the left-hand two threads from B). Put up pin b to the left of the weaver.

Continue to work the fan bringing in two threads from B at each of pins c, d and e. Leave out pairs after pins e, f, g and h. Turn the pillow back so that the edge is at the top. Remove pin B. Twist the pairs from b, c, d and e twice each. Bring the bobbins from A round to the working area and twist twice in pairs. Take the pair to the left of A as the weaver, and weave to the right to k, remembering the cloth stitch and twist edge stitches. Complete fan 2, bringing in pairs from b, c, d and e and leaving them out from the point as usual.

Turn the pillow to the former position. Hang eight pairs round pin C. Find the weaver to begin fan 3, bringing in the four pairs as in fan 1. Work as far as p leaving out pairs after pins m, n and o. Hang three pairs on D and complete fan 4 to q. Hang four pairs round E and work fan 5 to r.

Turn the pillow and remove pins C, D and E. Work cloth diamond 6 using pairs from fans 1 and 3. Put two twists on each pair and weave as in the illustration. Similarly the cloth diamond 7 is worked with pairs from fans 5 and 4. The spider 8 is worked next using pairs as indicated in the illustration, twist the 'legs' before and after the working.

Turn the pillow as before with the top to the left hand side. Continue. It will be necessary to hang three pairs on F for fan 9, and four pairs on G for fan 10. This completes the top edging and the pillow is turned to work the main part of the mat. Diamond 11 must be worked before all pairs are available for spider 12. Work fan 13 and continue normally.

Note that to achieve even half stitch on either side of shape 14, and to match 15 and 16, weaving must begin from the point in an outward direction. (on the left side to the left, and on the right side to the right). This ensures an equal number of diagonal threads as discussed on page 36. Notice too that the inner pinhole z has been used twice to maintain an even result. This method is an alternative to that given on page 47.

To complete the rectangular mat

Refer back to the beginning and to figure 54. The pillow was turned several times and the spiders and diamonds were worked as sufficient pairs became available. Of course it is possible to work all the fans and leave out all the pairs required for the spiders and diamonds before the pillow is turned. However this is not recommended, as the pairs become muddled and it is easier to work and understand the lace when working along a diagonal line. Similarly it is confusing if the mat is worked completely to the final edge fans, and it is difficult to cope with the large number of bobbins. The right side of the lace has been photographed, and therefore the fans appear to have been joined on the left instead of the right. Refer to figure 55 and work in the order indicated.

When the cloth diamond 16 has been completed press all the pins to the left of shapes 2, 7 and 8 into the pillow. Turn the pillow and, using the weaver from a, work fan 17 to f. Pairs will be left out after pins b, c, d and e. Hook pairs from diamond 16 into b and c. There will be four threads at each pinhole; knot them together and let them lie back out of the working area. Take threads from d and e

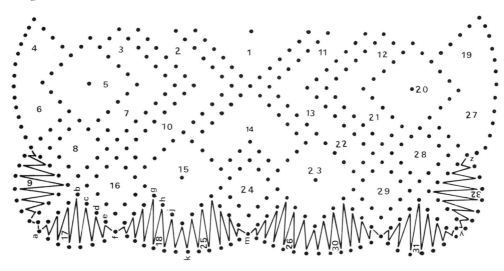

Fig 55 *Diagram for completing the rectangular mat*

and hook and knot them into the diamond, then let them lie back out of the working area. These will be sewn in later. It is to avoid bulkiness that they are distributed between the solid parts of the lace. Work fan 18 to k, bringing in pairs from 16, and leaving out pairs after g, h and j. The pairs from the spider will be hooked and knotted into these pinholes.

Turn the pillow and work from 19 to 24 inclusive. Again turn the pillow and work fan 25 to m; the legs from the spider will be brought in and pairs left out as in fan 17. Hook in and knot pairs as described for 16 and 17. Continue to work in the order given, turning the pillow as necessary, until fan 31 is complete. The pillow is turned so that the beginning of the mat is near to the lacemaker. Pins surrounding 19, 20, 27 and 28 must be pressed into the pillow. Fan 32 is worked from y to z. A join at the side will be less obvious than a corner join; also the corner receives harder use, so a join there should be avoided whenever possible. The mat is now complete.

To sew in threads when the work is complete
Take the threads lying along the edge of any shape and lay them along the edge in either direction to avoid thickness; for ease of handling these threads should be at least 10cm (4in) long. Certain threads are required to oversew these threads to the lace, and these should be left at least 30cm (12in) long. When the threads are secure, ends may be trimmed away; this is less unsightly than attempting to darn the threads into the actual lace. The roll of oversewn threads is neat and strong and on the wrong side of the finished article.

5 – Stitches and Variations

The majority of Torchon patterns adopt the same stitches and features; lace-makers will be conversant with those used in the early patterns in this book. However there are many others which can be introduced into new designs, or used to alter and add interest to existing patterns. The difference between an exciting and pleasing piece of lace and an insignificant disappointing result is dependent to a large extent upon the choice and combination of suitable shapes and stitches.

THE FOOTSIDE

The footside – or straight edge – which is sewn onto the fabric must be strong and straight. The usual method with one twisted passive pair is described on page 30; it is used in the first four patterns. The twists on the outer pair add strength, and more can be added if the thread is fine. In order to keep the footside edge straight it is necessary to retain the footside pins in position for as long as possible. If the lace is moved on the pillow, the pins must be replaced; if the card has been removed, the pins can be placed through the lace directly into the pillow. Special care should be taken when using a french pillow with a small roller.

If the lace is to be gathered, the threads of the twisted passive pair may be pulled to reduce fullness. To facilitate this, the passive pair may be left untwisted, but the weaver must be worked in the usual way. When preparing the pricking the ground and footside holes are equidistant; this makes it easy to reduce or increase the pattern width as desired. Refer to figure 56A.

Occasionally two pairs of twisted passives are included; these add strength and may improve a design. Refer to figure 165. When preparing the pricking, extra width is allowed between the footside and first row of ground holes. Refer to figure 56B and note that the footside holes are placed midway between the ground holes as usual but further away. In some patterns two or more straight pairs are incorporated – this is essential when working triangles or any lace where pairs are discarded into the footside. Refer to figures 100, 107 and 111. The collar in figure 129 has passives on the neck edge, and these are included to make a balanced pattern; here pairs are not discarded.

Tallies may be incorporated into the footside in two ways. The usual method is shown in figure 150, and the method for preparing a pricking is given in figure 56C. This method is also used to reduce the size of the neckline of the collar in figure 135. Tallies may be introduced as in figure 82, but this method is used only when a very definite square tally is required. The pricking is prepared as shown in figure 56D.

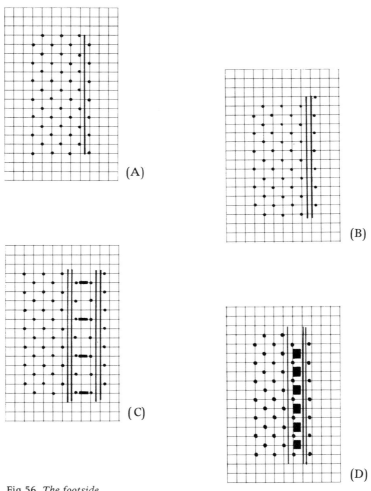

Fig 56 *The footside*

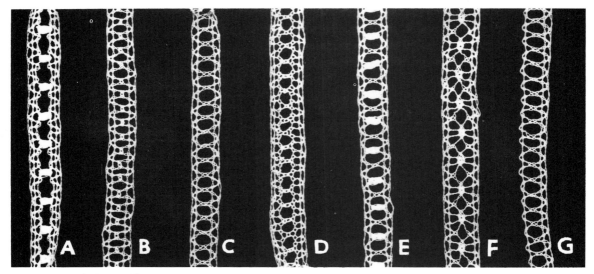

Fig 57 *Braids*

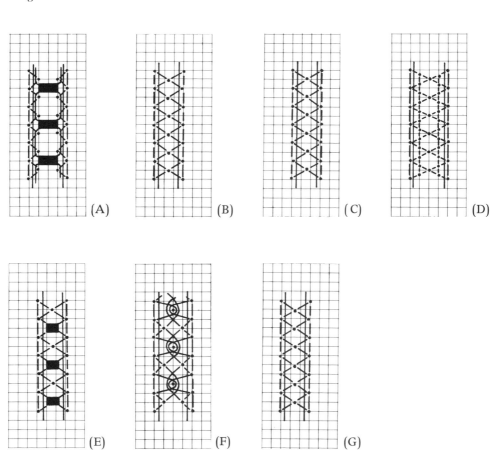

Fig 58 *Diagrams for the braids*

BRAIDS

It used to be normal practice to sew a narrow braid between the lace and the garment so that the lace was not damaged if removed for use elsewhere. A braid may be introduced to reduce the length on a curve, and is useful for children's collars. It is important to keep the pins in the lace as long as possible to achieve a firm, straight braid. Refer to figures 57 and 58.

Braid A

This is worked using eight pairs of bobbins. Set up a footside with two passive twisted pairs on both sides. Make tallies using the inner twisted passive pairs as indicated.

Braid B

This is the simplest of all the braids and consists of the normal Torchon footside on both edges. These are linked with cloth stitch and twist before and after a centre pin.

Braid C

The only difference between this braid and the previous one is that half stitch is worked before and after the centre pin.

Braid D

A more complicated and wider braid, this has the normal footside, but all the other pins are worked with half stitch with an extra twist before and after the pin. The illustration clarifies the direction of the threads.

Braid E

Very like braid C, this pattern alternates the covered pin with a tally which requires no pin. Unlike braid A it is the weaver which makes the tally.

Braid F

Eight pairs are required, the second pair for the spider on either side come from the footside.

Braid G

This pattern has the footside on one edge only and lends itself readily to a curved edge. It is similar to C.

Application

When using coloured threads, braids may provide decorative trimmings for lampshades or other furnishings. Braid F is attractive when used as an insertion in the front of a blouse, or when made in coarse thread and attached around a full skirt. Some braids can be mounted on velvet and used as chokers; others are suitable for baby clothes.

GROUND

The ground – or net – is used as a background stitch to cover an area quickly; it is usually insignificant in appearance to emphasise the pattern features. When working Torchon ground, the pins are always covered using the same stitch before and after the pin. Normally half stitches are used; refer to figures 10 and 148.

The effect obtained by using cloth stitch and twist is shown in figures 28 and 161. More variety can be added with tallies, see figures 28 and 84. The ground is worked in an unusual way in the collar in figure 123, and the whole pattern is dependent upon the arrangement of tallies. This idea may be used in the normal diagonal method of working; refer to figure 90. Blocks of cloth stitch are sometimes included to reduce the area of ground, and, as in figure 167, they may become an integral part of the pattern.

Rose grounds are elaborate, varied and attractive, the method of working is common to all types and they are easy to work. Torchon honeycomb can also be used as ground, and it is seen most commonly in Scandinavian laces. It is shown in the centre of the cloth in figure 153, and directions for working accompany it in figure 154.

ROSE GROUND SAMPLER

The insertion sampler, figure 59, gives six varieties of rose ground, all based on the same arrangement of pins. This sampler may be used as a pattern by selecting one rose ground and one diamond filling.

To begin

Hang two pairs of bobbins round every pin along the top edge, and then hang one extra pair on the pins at both ends. Twist the two threads falling either side of every pin twice each. Take the two outside bobbins on the left-hand pin, and work to the right through all the pairs as far as the last two pairs and stop. Twist the right-hand two threads and work these two pairs together in cloth stitch and twist to cover the pin. The inner pair (ie ignore the outer right-hand pair and use the next) becomes the weaver, and weaves through the pair which has travelled across and on through all the other pairs except the last left-hand pair. The working diagram figure 61, explains the method clearly.

The gimp thread

The use of gimp threads has been discussed on page 39, and the path of the gimp thread is shown in the diagram. However the gimp thread must be firm at x. When the cloth diamond has been completed, enclose it with the gimp thread by bringing it to the left through six pairs which hang from the diamond. Twist each pair twice and pull the gimp firmly. Carefully bring the gimp back through three pairs and twist these pairs twice more. Note that only one pair of gimp threads is necessary, and that one thread encloses the cloth shapes on both sides to avoid a centre hole. If necessary refer back to figure 29.

Fig 59 *Rose ground sampler*

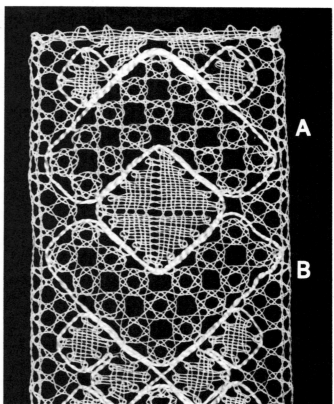

Fig 60 *Top of the sampler*

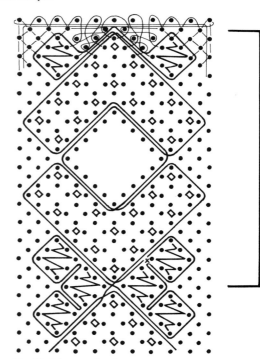

Fig 61 *Diagram for figure 60*

Fig 62 *Diagram for working rose ground units*

Working the rose ground

Refer to figure 62 for all six sets of instructions. It is worked in four pin units, each completed separately. Each unit requires four pairs, two from the right and two from the left and all must be available before starting to work. Always a stitch is worked on either side before the unit is begun. Similarly stitches are worked on either side immediately after it is complete. No pins are used for these stitches; they are indicated as ringed letters, a, b, g and h on the diagram. Pinholes c, d, e and f are worked using the same stitch before and after the pin. When working several rose ground units, if the stitch indicated by a ringed letter has been worked at the completion of one unit, it is not worked a second time for the next unit. Refer to figures 60 to 65.

Fig 63 *Centre of the sampler*   Fig 64 *Bottom of the sampler*

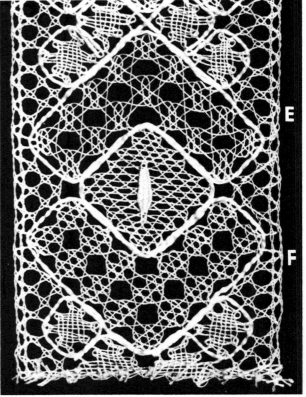

Rose ground A

(1) a, using two pairs from left work cloth stitch and twist.
(2) b, using two pairs from right work cloth stitch and twist.
(3) centre pairs work half stitch, pin c, half stitch.
(4) left pairs work half stitch, pin d, half stitch.
(5) right pairs work half stitch, pin e, half stitch.
(6) centre pairs work half stitch, pin f, half stitch.
(7) g, using left-hand pairs work cloth stitch and twist.
(8) h, using right-hand pairs work cloth stitch and twist.

Rose ground B

(1) a, using two pairs from left work half stitch.
(2) b, using two pairs from right work half stitch.
(3) centre pairs work half stitch, pin c, half stitch.
(4) left pairs work half stitch, pin d, half stitch.
(5) right pairs work half stitch, pin e, half stitch.
(6) centre pairs work half stitch, pin f, half stitch.
(7) g, using left-hand pairs work half stitch.
(8) h, using right-hand pairs work half stitch.

Rose ground C

(1) a, using two pairs from left work cloth stitch and twist.
(2) b, using two pairs from right work cloth stitch and twist.
(3) centre pairs work cloth stitch and twist, pin c, cloth stitch and twist.
(4) left-hand pairs work cloth stitch and twist, pin d, cloth stitch and twist.
(5) right-pairs work cloth stitch and twist, pin e, cloth stitch and twist.
(6) centre pairs work cloth stitch and twist, pin f, cloth stitch and twist.
(7) g, using left-hand pairs work cloth stitch and twist.
(8) h, using right-hand pairs work cloth stitch and twist.

Rose ground D

(1) a, using left-hand pairs work cloth stitch and twist.
(2) b, using right-hand pairs work cloth stitch and twist.
(3) centre pairs work half stitch. Consider the right hand of these two pairs the weaver and give it one twist extra.
(4) Put up pin c, weave to the left through the other pair at c and the left hand pair.
(5) Twist the weaver once more and put up pin d. Weave to the right through all three pairs, twist the weaver once more and put up pin e.
(6) Weave back through two pairs only, (one pair was left out after d), and twist the weaver once more. Put up pin f and cover with half stitch.
(7) g, using the left hand pairs work cloth stitch and twist.
(8) h, using the right hand pairs work cloth stitch and twist.

Rose ground E

The pinholes d and e are not used.
(1) a, using left pairs work half stitch.

(2) b, using the right pairs work half stitch.
(3) centre pairs work half stitch, pin c, half stitch.
(4) left-hand pairs work half stitch.
(5) right-hand pairs work half stitch.
(6) centre pairs work half stitch, pin f, half stitch.
(7) g, using left hand pairs work half stitch.
(8) h, using right hand pairs work half stitch.

Fig 65 *Diagram for Rose Ground F*

Rose ground F

This filling is worked in a continuous diagonal line. Refer to figure 65.

(1) Work half stitches with pairs to enter work at a and c, e and g, etc, also pairs to enter at a and b.
(2) Work the half stitch trail as shown in the illustration, then make half stitches with pairs from b and d, f and h, etc.
(3) Continue with the next half stitch trail.

To complete the work

Work as far as possible, then tie the pairs together with reef knots.

SPIDERS

The sampler in figure 66 shows several spider forms which may provide variety when planning patterns. Instructions are given for each form and should be used with the accompanying illustrations.

Fig 66 *Sampler showing seven types of spiders*

Large spider (A)

Refer to figures 67 and 68. This spider is in common use. The number of pairs used to make it vary; in this case five pairs enter on each side, whereas in the Spanish pattern (figure 20) only three pairs enter on each side. However the principle is always the same. An equal number of pairs on either side of centre are required; there will never be a pair directly above the centre spider pin. Isolate the pairs to be used. Pins with brightly coloured heads may be placed on either side to hold other pairs out of the working area. Twist the pairs to be used for the spider three times each and find the centre. Take the pair to the left of centre and weave through all the pairs to the right of centre in cloth stitch, in this case five pairs.

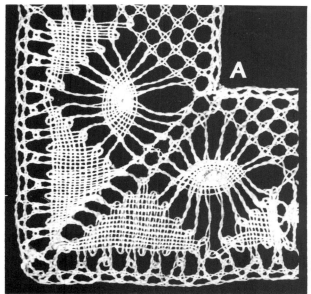

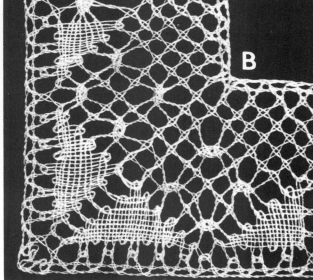

Fig 67 *Large spider*

Fig 69 *Small spiders*

Fig 68 *Diagram for figure 67*

Fig 70 *Diagram for figure 69*

Take the next pair to the left of centre and weave to the right through the same number of pairs, in this case five; it will lie alongside the previous pair but not pass through it. Continue until all pairs have followed through and lie flat in the same order alongside each other. Place a pin between the centre pairs in the middle pinhole. Repeat the above instructions, beginning with the pair to the left of the centre pin and working to the right. Nothing is twisted at the centre, it is important to keep the 'body' flat, and no movements are reversed. When complete, the pairs are twisted before continuing with the rest of the pattern.

Small spider (B)

Refer to figures 69 and 70. The pattern consists of small spiders separated by rows of Torchon ground. Work the small spider using pairs from a and b, and v and w. Work half stitch, pin, half stitch ground stitches from c with the left side two pairs from the spider. Work half stitch, pin, half stitch ground from x with the right side two pairs from the spider. Pairs meet to work pin o in the same manner as the other ground pins. Continue following the working diagram.

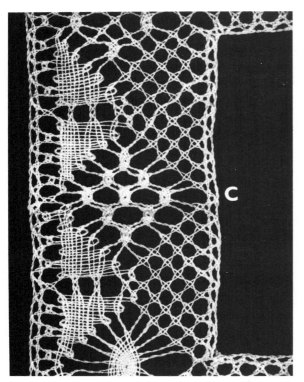

Fig 71 *Compound spider*

Fig 72 *Diagram for figure 71*

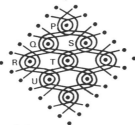

Fig 73 *Open-centred spider*

Fig 74 *Diagram for figure 73*

Compound spider (C)

At first this may appear confusing, but with reference to figures 71 and 72, it is seen to be similar to the previous spider form but without the ground stitches. Spider P is worked with pairs from left and right as in the previous pattern. Spider Q is worked with two pairs from the left and the two pairs from spider P. Spider R is worked with two pairs from the left and two from spider Q. Spider S is worked with two pairs from the right and two pairs from spider P. Spider T is worked with pairs from spiders Q and S, and spider U is worked with pairs from spiders R and T. Continue.

Open-centred spider (D)

This is a very useful alternative, and more attractive than the large spider shown in A. Figures 73 and 74 explain the method of working. Three pairs are crossed in the usual way and the fourth pair becomes a weaver passing through the three pairs on its own side to the appropriate centre pin and back to work half stitch, pin, half stitch with the fifth pair. It travels back to the centre and out again before the three original pairs cross each other to complete the effect. (See figure 82.)

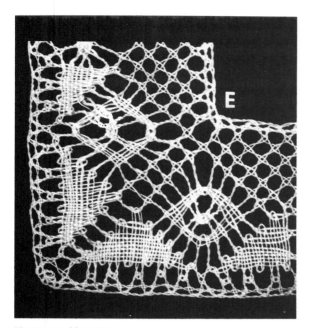

Fig 75 *Double spider*

Fig 76 *Diagram for figure 75*

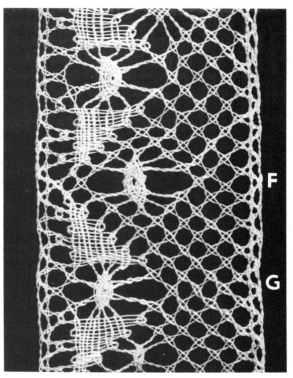

Fig 77 *Weaver-legged spider and spider within cloth*

Fig 78 *Diagram for spider within cloth*

Double spider (E)
This is another useful variation when there are five pairs available and the large spider A seems too large for the particular design. Figures 75 and 76 explain the working.

Weaver-legged spider (F)
Other forms are occasionally found in old lace, particularly where pairs enter and become weavers, one effect is shown in figure 77. Another is used in the edging shown in figures 79 and 80.

Spider within cloth (G)
Refer to figures 77 and 78. Pairs leaving the cloth are twisted to form four legs, two for each side. These and one additional pair from the ground on each side are used in the normal way. Care must be taken to ensure that the pairs leaving and re-entering the cloth are well positioned.

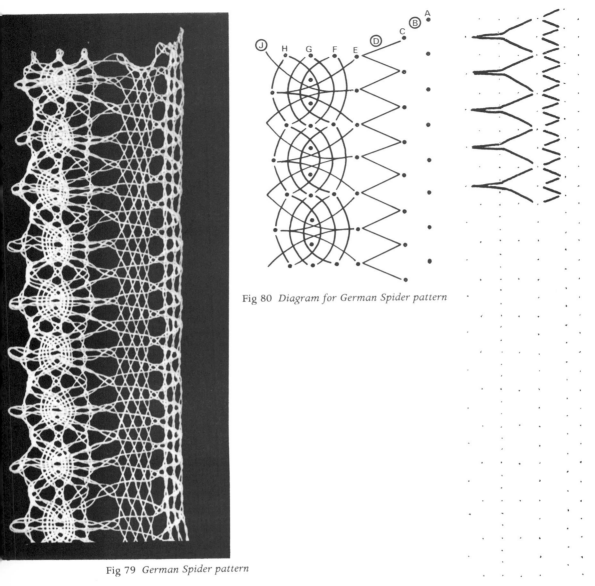

Fig 80 *Diagram for German Spider pattern*

Fig 79 *German Spider pattern*

Fig 81 *Pricking for German Spider pattern*

GERMAN SPIDER PATTERN

Refer to figures 79, 80 and 81. This edging lends itself to a curved footside more readily than most; when the twisted passive pairs are pulled the pattern can be used in a variety of ways. It is not an easy pattern to master, but once understood it is quick to make. However, the initial trial sample requires care and concentration. It can be divided into three parts: footside, half stitch trail, and spider edging. The half stitch trail is straightforward and uses the same number of pairs throughout; the weaver links with the footside on the right, and the spider pairs on the left at every pinhole.

Method of working

Hang two pairs round A and work the usual cloth stitch and twist. Hang two pairs on a support pin B and work through in cloth stitch and twist; these will be the passive pairs. Hang one pair on a support pin to work half stitch, pin C, half stitch. The right-hand pair will return to the footside and the left-hand pair will become the half stitch trail weaver. Hang three pairs on a support pin D for the trail, and work through them in half stitch. Hang one more pair behind in order to work half stitch, pin E, half stitch. The right-hand pair is the half stitch trail weaver and the left-hand pair will enter the spider later. Hang two pairs round each of pins F, G and H and in each case cover with cloth stitch and twist. The pairs from H and G, and G and F work cloth stitch, and the pairs from F and E work cloth stitch and twist. A pair should be hung on a support pin J to work cloth and twist with the other pair from H; no pin is used and care is necessary to avoid pulling this pair out of position. Follow the working diagram, and remember that there are no twists in the centre of the spider. If difficulty is experienced, make a tracing of the diagram using coloured crayons, and work the lace in coloured threads.

HEART AND SPIDER PATTERN

Reference was made to this pattern when discussing the variations which can be worked on the footside, however instructions were left until the spider had been mastered. Refer to figures 82 and 83.

Fig 82 *Heart and Spider pattern*

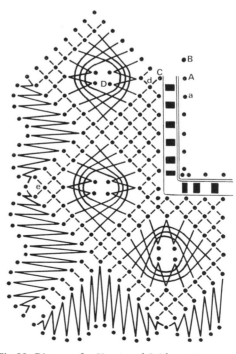

Fig 83 *Diagram for Heart and Spider pattern*

Method of working

Begin with the footside. Hang two pairs on A and three pairs on C. On a support pin at B hang two pairs in order, these will be footside passive pairs. Twist the two right-hand threads on pin A, and work cloth stitch and twist to cover the pin. Ignore the right-hand pair as usual and work to the left with the other pair through the two pairs hanging from B. These pairs are always worked in cloth stitch and remain untwisted throughout. Take the two right-hand threads on pin C and twist twice, then work to the left through the other two pairs on the same pin in cloth stitch and twist. This pair continues to the left into the ground, and works a cloth stitch and twist with a pair hung on a support pin at D. Pin d is put up diagonally from C and covered with cloth stitch and twist. More pairs are hung on support pins and the diagonal row of ground completed to e. This pattern is worked using the cloth stitch and twist ground stitch throughout.

There are still two pairs hanging on pin C, the middle pair remains in this position to become a twisted passive pair, and the right-hand pair is required for the tally. This pair, which is always the fifth pair from the right, and the pair which has worked through from the footside pin (the fourth pair from the edge) together make the tally. Both pairs must be twisted twice. The second thread becomes the weaver and the tally is worked according to the instructions given on page 40.

When the tally is complete it is advisable to leave the weaver on the right-hand side. The left-hand side of the tally works cloth and twist with the pair to the left, ie the twisted passive pair, and then continues to the left with ground stitches. The right-hand pair from the tally works to the right with cloth stitch through the two passive pairs, is twisted, and the footside pin is worked. The pair which comes back through the passive pairs is ready for the next tally.

Another variation is to have two sets of passive cloth pairs, instead of one twisted and one in cloth. Figure 56 shows the arrangement of pinholes for these variations, D as explained above and C with the second set of cloth passive pairs. Continue as above to complete the pattern.

6 – Beginning and Ending

Two of the chief problems encountered by lacemakers are how to begin and how to complete the work neatly. This section shows how to solve or simplify the difficulties, and explains methods for a variety of situations. Each method is explained with reference to a particular pattern and, once understood, other prickings may be adapted and repricked to be worked in the same way. Mats, square or rectangular, collars and triangles all require a neat beginning and ending, and these methods are discussed elsewhere in this book.

In order to learn the basic principles of Torchon lace, and to understand the beginning, it is recommended that lace is started along a diagonal line. Refer to the patterns on pages 30, 42, 46, 75 and 130. If a length of lace is to be joined, it will be less obvious if the threads are sewn in along a line of working. The method for beginning is given on page 30.

GETTING RID OF KNOTS

Always prepare pairs of bobbins which are coupled with no visible knot. If the thread is newly wound onto bobbins, wind as much as possible onto one bobbin, take the end, and wind half of the thread back onto the second bobbin. If the bobbins have been used previously and therefore have ends, knot pairs together, remove the hitch from one bobbin and wind the knot back onto the neck of the bobbin. Replace the hitch. The knot will not be included in the lace, but a new thread will be introduced later.

To get rid of knots in the work, take one bobbin and secure the thread to a support pin outside the work; bring the thread through to lie alongside the thread with the knot, then fasten the bobbins together with a rubber band, or the kind of covered wire twist which is normally used for closing plastic bags. Work the threads as one, and discard the knotted thread before the knot enters the lace. It is usual to do this when the knot is 10–12cm (4–5in) from the lace. The threads are worked double for approximately 2.5cm (1in), but this will depend on the closeness of the stitches.

COMPLETING THE LACE

Place the beginning onto the pricking and put all the pins in for at least 25mm (1in), more on the headside and footside. Place a piece of clear plastic over the lace and pins, to keep the work clean and facilitate working, and continue the lace until all the pinholes have been worked. It is obvious where the pairs should work the next stitch, and it is into this position that they are hooked to join the lace. Take a fine crochet hook, ascertain that the pair has the required number of twists, remove the pin at the beginning of the lace, hook one thread through and put the second thread through the loop. Pull both bobbins carefully, tie one knot to hold the threads firmly and replace the pin. Repeat, moving only one pin at a time, and hook and knot all the pairs into the correct position.

Cut the threads, leaving about 300mm (12in) of thread on the extreme right-hand pair, and 75mm (3in) on the other threads. Use one of the long threads to oversew the passive threads along the footside. Take the short threads, other than the passive threads which have already been sewn in, and roll them together along the diagonal line. Use the other long thread to overcast these threads closely onto the diagonal line. As this is done on the wrong side of the work it will show very little. However it is more important to achieve a strong join that will withstand wear and laundering than an invisible join that frays and falls apart.

BEGINNING ON A STRAIGHT LINE AT RIGHT ANGLES TO THE FOOTSIDE

First method

The simplest way of beginning on a straight line has been shown in the Rose Ground Sampler on page 58. This may be adapted for other patterns with ground. The pairs are hung round pins along a straight line. It is important that the pairs are round the pin, lying one inside the other, and not as pairs side by side. The pins are not covered, and the threads on each side of the pin move diagonally to complete the ground stitches or other features below.

If the simple beginning described above has been used, the ends of the lace will be hidden in a seam, a hem or a binding. The lace should be worked until all the pins along a straight line have been completed, and then pairs are tied together with reef knots, and the ends are cut off.

Second method

Refer to figure 84 which shows the beginning and ending as a footside. The pricking is given in figure 85. Notice the working of the trails to give the effect of continuity when seen at a distance. Figures 86 and 87 show the detailed beginning. Hang four pairs round pin A. Work cloth stitch and twist with the two right-hand pairs. Work cloth stitch and twist with the centre pairs. The pair on the right-hand side is the outside footside pair and the next pair is the passive twisted pair for the footside. The third pair from the right is the passive twisted pair for the top edge.

Put up pin B to the right of the extreme left-hand pair. Hang two pairs round

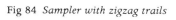

Fig 84 *Sampler with zigzag trails*

Fig 85 *Pricking for figure 84*

Fig 86 *Beginning the sampler*

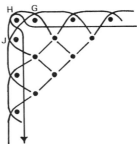
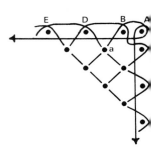

Fig 87 *Diagram for figure 86*

pin B to fall close to the pin, leaving the original left-hand pair to the left. Work this pair and the two threads to the left of pin B together in cloth stitch and twist. Of these three pairs, the left-hand pair is the outside pair for the top edge, the right-hand pair works cloth stitch and twist twice to the right through both new passive pairs and is twisted before working cloth stitch and twist with the outside pair, the footside pin C is put up inside both pairs, the outer pair is ignored and the inner pair works through the passive pair to cover the pin. The usual footside is set into position. The centre pair at pin B (ie the second pair from the left) works with the pair to the right (the top passive pair) and is ready for the first ground pin a.

Pin D is put to the right of the left-hand edge pair and two pairs hung round it as for pin B. The left-hand pairs work cloth stitch and twist, the left-hand pair remains at the edge and the other pairs in turn (right-hand pair first) work cloth stitch and twist through the passive pair. Introduce two new pairs at pin E in the same way and continue similarly along the top edge.

The last two pairs are introduced at pin G, the left-hand pair remains on the outside for the corner, and the other pairs work through the passives as previously described. The top passive pair works cloth stitch and twist with the top outside pair (the two left-hand pairs work together) and pin H, the corner pin, is put to the right of both pairs. The left-hand pair is ignored and the next pairs work cloth

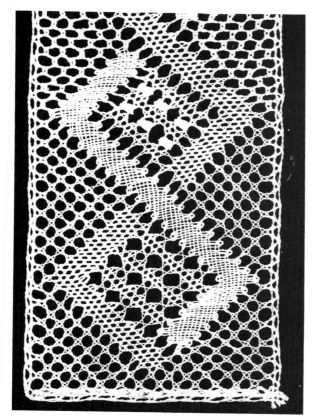

Fig 88 *Completing the sampler*

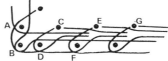

Fig 89 *Diagram for figure 88*

stitch and twist to cover the pin. The left-hand pairs work cloth stitch and twist and pin J is put up to the right of them. The left-hand pair is ignored and the next pairs work cloth stitch and twist to cover the pin. Taking the pairs from the top, the ground may be worked. Always bring pairs into the work diagonally.

To complete the lace, refer to figures 88 and 89. Complete the lace until only the bottom row of holes remains. Three pairs will hang at either side and two from each ground pin. When pin A has been completed, the twisted passive pair (ie the second pair from the left) works with the edge pair in cloth stitch and twist and the corner pin B is put up to the right of these two pairs. The outer pair remains as the footside pair along the bottom edge and the other pair lies alongside to become a passive pair. The other pair from A also lies in position as a passive pair.

The pairs from ground are worked as follows; the complication lies in the number of pairs to be managed rather than difficult lace stitches. Attention must be given to achieving good tension as so many pairs of bobbins are to be discarded. Two pairs hang from pin C; ascertain that the half stitch after the pin has been worked accurately. The left-hand pair from pin C works to the left through the next two pairs (the passives) in cloth stitch. It is twisted once, and works cloth stitch and twist with the outside pair. Pin D is put up to the right of these two pairs as a footside pin. Ignore the outer (left-hand) pair and work a cloth stitch to cover pin D.

Allow the right-hand pair from pin C to lie alongside the passive pairs. The left-hand pair from pin E works to the left through all the passive pairs (four pairs) in cloth stitch, it is twisted once and works cloth stitch and twist with the outside pair and pin F is put in position inside (to the right of) two pairs. The outer pair is ignored and the other pair works cloth stitch to cover the pin. Discard the two pairs of passives next to the right. To do this, take the bobbins and pull the threads back to the left to lie between pins A and B. Do not cut the threads yet as the bobbins will keep the threads taut and maintain the tension. Allow the right-hand pair from E to lie as a passive thread. Take the left-hand pair from pin G and continue.

At each ground pin the left-hand pair works four cloth stitches to the left; it is twisted and the outside pin is worked and covered. Two pairs are discarded and the other pair is unworked but joins the passive pairs.

Finally the passives and edge pairs are worked in cloth stitch through all remaining pairs and tied firmly with reef knots.

In this sample piece of lace a variety of Torchon stitches and fillings are used, also both half stitch and cloth stitch and twist grounds. Tallies are also used in different ways; see figure 84.

The group of four tallies in ground is worked within the normal arrangement of ground holes; refer to figure 90. Work the complete row of ground stitches from footside pin A. Work the second row of stitches from pin B as far as, but not including, pin c. Use pairs from a and b to make the tally and end with the weaver on the left-hand side. Work ground pins c and d and complete the row. It is important to leave the tally weaver on the left; if the centre and one side threads from the tally are anchored into position before the weaver, the weaver is less likely to get pulled and the tally distorted.

The group of three tallies show larger tallies and in this case the tallies are worked instead of ground stitches. Refer to figure 91. Work the complete row of ground stitches from footside pin A. Work the second row from pin B as far as, and including, pin b. Work the third row of ground stitches as far as, and including, pin x. Use pairs from a and b to make the tally, leaving the weaver on the left-hand side. Work ground stitches d and c and e, in that order. The pairs from f and c work the next tally. As the tally replaces a ground stitch, it is the pairs that would normally make the ground stitch that are used for the tally.

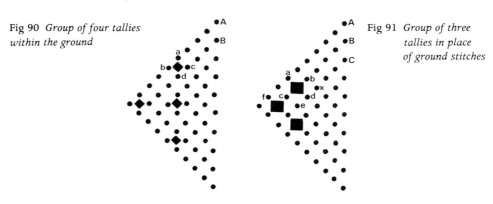

Fig 90 *Group of four tallies within the ground*

Fig 91 *Group of three tallies in place of ground stitches*

SAMPLER WITH LACE EXTENSIONS

It is possible to work an extension of lace at either end for strength and as a means of securing the ends. Using this method, the pattern is designed so that the ends may be extended and folded back as an invisible overlap. Refer to figure 92. The cloth triangles may be folded back and sewn down. This may seem to be unnecessary at the beginning, but it is essential at the end to secure the threads, and it is preferable that both ends are similar.

Fig 92 *Sampler with lace extensions*

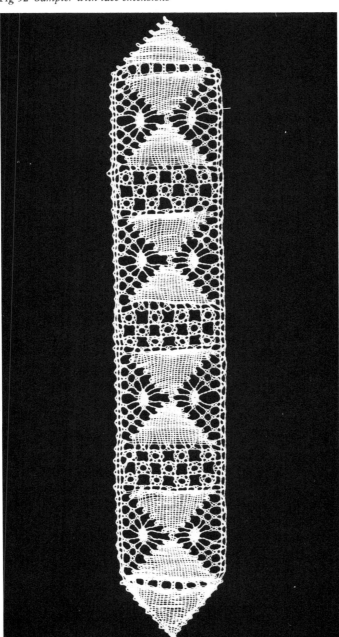

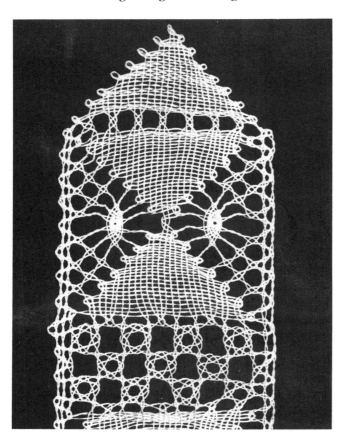

Fig 93 *The top extension*

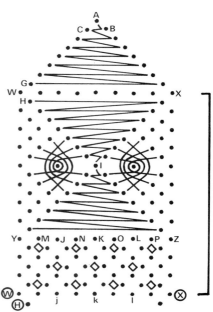

Fig 94 *Diagram for figure 93*

To begin

Refer to figures 93 and 94. Hang two pairs round the top pin A. Twist the right-hand threads twice and work a cloth stitch to cover the pin. On either side hang pairs on support pins behind the work. Work the cloth triangle as follows. Take the right-hand pair from the top covered pin A and work through the next pair (on a support pin) to the right in cloth stitch. Put up pin B to the left of the weaver. Work back through the two pairs in the work and through one more pair (on a support pin) to the left. Put up pin C to the right of the weaver. Continue, bringing in one pair at each pin as far as and including G. Cover pin G with a cloth stitch. Take the left-hand pair from G and work to the left through two pairs from a support pin. These two pairs become twisted passive pairs on the headside. The pin W is put up to the right of the weaver only, which works in cloth and twist through the two passive pairs and is ready to continue the cloth. Using the same number of pairs, a footside with one twisted passive pair could be worked here if desired.

The right-hand pair works to the right through two more pairs from a support pin and pin X is put up to the left of two pairs. The outer pair is ignored and pin X is covered. The footside is set into position; there is one passive pair. At this stage the pairs in the cloth triangle are twisted once each. The three pairs at either edge are ignored, and the adjacent pairs are worked together in a half stitch. Pins are put up to keep them in position, and half stitches worked to cover the pins. To begin the second triangle the third and fourth pairs from the left work a cloth stitch, pin H is placed between the pairs. The pair to the left of pin H becomes the weaver and the cloth stitch is worked as in the illustration. Pairs must be left out after every pin for the ground and the spider. When pin I has been covered, the ground and spider are worked.

To set the rose ground into position

When the cloth has been completed, also the head pin Y and footside pin Z, twist the pairs from the cloth once each. Find the centre pairs and work half stitch, pin K, half stitch. Ignore the next two pairs to the left, and the next two pairs work a half stitch, pin J, half stitch. Ignore the two pairs to the right of pin K and use the next two pairs to work a half stitch, pin L, half stitch.

To work pin M, which is the first pin in a rose ground unit, proceed as follows. Ascertain that pin Y has been worked and that the weaver is the third pair from the left. Take this pair and the fourth pair from the left and work cloth stitch and twist; this is the equivalent to a in figure 62. Take the next pairs to the right (ie one pair from the cloth and the left-hand pair from J) and work cloth stitch and twist; this is equivalent to b in the same illustration. Now the unit may be worked beginning with half stitch, pin M, half stitch. Remember to complete the unit with the stitches labelled g and h in figure 62.

To work the unit beginning with pin N, proceed as follows. Take one pair from J and one from the cloth to work cloth stitch and twist; these pairs are the left-hand side pairs for the unit. Take one pair from the cloth and one pair from K to work a cloth stitch and twist; these are the right hand side pairs for the unit. Commence with half stitch, pin N, half stitch and work the unit. Work the unit beginning at pin O similarly. Before working the unit beginning with pin P, ascertain that the footside pin Z has been completed, and that the weaver lies third from the edge. When all rose ground units are complete, work the footside pins W and X, which are ringed in figure 94. As the units have been fully worked it will be necessary only to select the pairs to work pins j, k and l in half stitch, pin, half stitch. The cloth triangle working begins with pin H.

To complete the work

Refer to figure 95. The line of pins enclosed with half stitch, pin, half stitch, is worked in the same way as the beginning. The weaver continues in cloth stitch and is twisted as it passes round the pin. There are no passive pairs and no straight edge. When the weaver has worked across the cloth triangle twice in each direction and lies on the left side of the work, discard the penultimate pair on either side. Each time the weaver returns to this position, discard the penultimate pairs, thus reducing the number of pairs in the cloth. When the last pin is placed in position there are eight pairs left at the bottom. As long as the number of pairs has been reduced, the final number is unimportant. These pairs are plaited together and the plait is turned back and sewn inside the double triangle.

Fig 95 *The bottom extension*

To plait more than two pairs

Take the left-hand pair and work through the remaining pairs in half stitch; pull the pair well to the side to keep the work as close as possible. Take the left-hand pair and work through in half stitch. Continue repeating this movement across the work from left to right until a plait of the required length is achieved. Tie the outside threads on each side together, then trim the ends.

LACE WITH PATTERNED ENDS

Consideration must be given to designing patterns or adapting existing patterns so that the edge features are an integral part of the ends as well as the edge. The sample shown in figure 96 can be extended with more pattern repeats for use as a cuff, or for the ends of place mats, pillow cases or guest towels. As the right side of the lace is underneath (ie close to the pricking card) when working, the discarded threads are cut off or sewn on the top, which is the wrong side of the work. The photograph shows the right side of the work, and is therefore apparently a reversal of figure 97.

Planning and pricking the pattern

Figure 98 shows how the pattern is worked out on graph paper, the cloth triangles are repeated from the corner and the exact width of the pricking is controlled by the triangles along the side. The gimp feature is copied in position between the triangles.

To begin

Refer to figure 97. Hang two pairs on pin A and two pairs on pin B. Twist the threads to the right of each pin twice each. Using the left-hand pair from A work

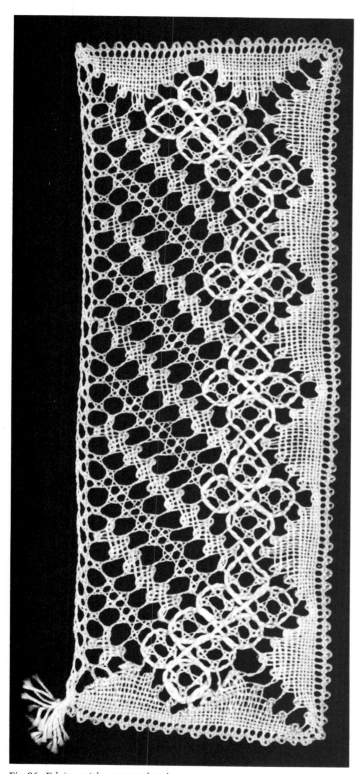

Fig 96 *Edging with patterned ends*

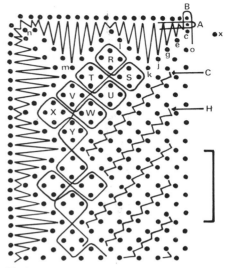

Fig 97 *Diagram for figure 96*

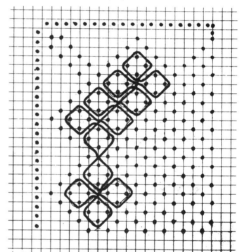

Fig 98 *Planning the pattern*

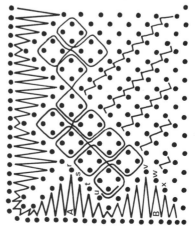

Fig 99 *Completing the lace*

cloth stitch twice to the left through the pairs on B. Similarly work two cloth stitches through using the other pair from A. Turn the pillow so that the footside is at the top. Hang two pairs on a support pin outside the work at X and allow all four threads to fall to the left of the right-hand pair in the work. Take the third pair from the left (ie the left-hand pair from B) and work one cloth stitch with the two threads from the left of pin X. Put up pin c between the pairs and take the right-hand pair as weaver; cover the pin and continue to the left through the next pair in cloth stitch, then twist the weaver once and work cloth stitch and twist with the outside edge pair. This pair is now established as weaver for the triangle. Cover the pin with cloth stitch and twist and work cloth stitch through the three pairs in the triangle.

Remove pin x to allow the pairs to fall into position in the work. Replace pin x and hang two more pairs on the pin. Work the triangle weaver through the two threads to the left of pin x, put up pin e and work back to the cloth stitch and twist edge. Introduce new pairs at g, j and k. Turn the pillow so that the footside is on the right side. The pair at c will become the twisted footside passive, and the right-hand pair is the outer footside pair. The pair from e is twisted and works the footside stitch at o. Pairs from g, j and k are twisted and used as required. Turn the pillow and complete the triangle leaving out pairs after pins k to l inclusive. Work the next triangle joining in at each pin as far as m, in the same way as pairs were joined in from c to k. Work to n, leaving out pairs after pins m to n. Turn the pillow and proceed in the usual way, this method of beginning is similar to the method for the rectangular mats.

The gimp thread
Only one pair is required and the method of working is the same as in figure 26. In this pattern the order of working the rings is indicated in letter order. Note that the one thread encircles all the rings.

Cloth stitch and half stitch diagonal trails
This is a strong and attractive alternative to ground stitches. The pairs from the gimp enclosed circles are given three twists each and the diagonal of cloth worked as in the illustration. The pairs from this trail are twisted three times and the half stitch trail worked as in the illustration. The cloth trail is indicated as C and the half stitch trail as H.

To complete the strip
Study the instructions for the completion of the rectangular mat on page 52. This pattern is worked in the same way. Refer to figure 99. Turn the pillow so that the footside is at the bottom. Work triangle A. Pairs from r, s, t and u will be sewn into triangle A as described for the rectangular mat. Similarly pairs from v, w, x and the footside will be sewn into triangle B. The remaining pairs will be tied in a bundle, as described for the triangular insertion on page 85.

7 – Triangles

Triangles may be designed as an extension of the corner for an edging or for use as insertion. The insertion will be considered first, it is fairly quick to make and requires comparatively short lengths of thread, so it may be worthwhile to use up the threads remaining on the bobbins after a larger piece of work has been completed.

ROSE GROUND TRIANGLE

Preparation

To design or copy a triangle, work using graph paper with the lines running horizontally and vertically. Refer to the triangle in figure 100; the longest side, Z, is the true footside and the pricking is worked out accordingly. Mark alternate intersections down a vertical line for the footside pins. As there are several passive pairs it is necessary to allow space for these and the first row of ground pins are placed two squares from the footside. Sides X and Y are worked to give the appearance of a footside, so that the three edges look the same. Pairs are introduced into the pattern from side X; they work diagonally to side Z and back to be discarded on side Y. Refer to figure 101.

The same number of passive pairs are introduced for sides X and Z and these remain unchanged; however, all the pairs are gradually discarded on side Y, and it is necessary to have adequate space and passive pairs to do this as unobtrusively as possible. Figure 102 shows the arrangement of the footside pinholes for side X, and figure 103 shows the arrangement for the point and side Y. The pricking may be worked out from the photograph using the three small illustrations as a guide, however a pricking is also included in figure 104.

To begin

Refer to the photograph and figure 102. Hang eight pairs round pin A, twist the two right-hand pairs (these are not true pairs but threads falling side by side) twice each, and work them together with a cloth stitch and two twists on each pair. This stitch, cloth stitch and two twists instead of the usual one twist, is used

81

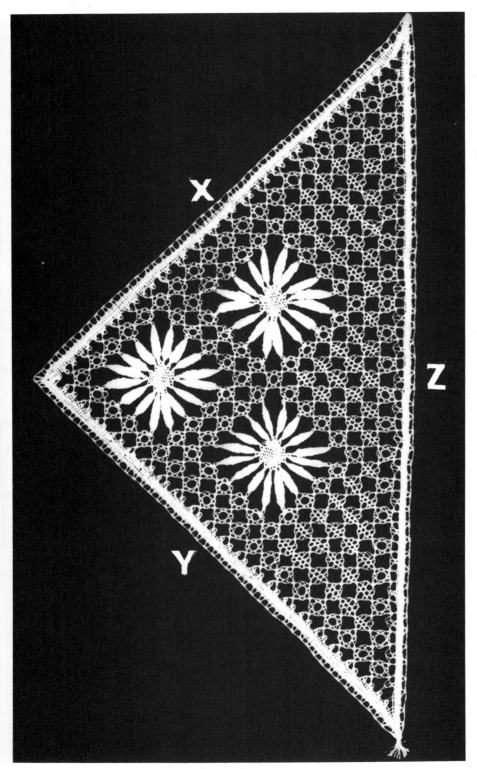

Fig 100 *Rose Ground Triangle*

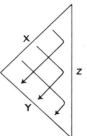

Fig 101 *Direction of working the triangle*

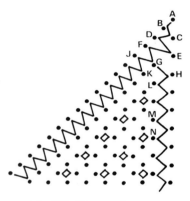

Fig 102 *Diagram for Rose Ground Triangle*

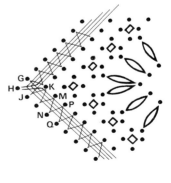

Fig 103 *The arrangement of the point*

Fig 104 *Pricking for Rose Ground Triangle*

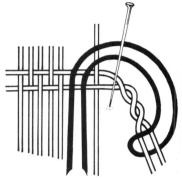

Fig 105 *Placing the new thread under the weaver*

Fig 106 *Completing the triangle*

on the footside in this pattern. There is no pin to put up, but the right-hand pair is ignored, and the left-hand pair works to the left in cloth stitch as far as the last pair. Twist the weaver and the outside pair twice each and work them together with cloth stitch and two twists. Remember that both pairs are given two twists.

Put up pin B to the right of both pairs, ignore the left-hand pair and work as far as the last pair on the right-hand side using the other pair. Twist the weaver twice; there will be two twists on the edge pair. Do *not* work the footside stitch but put up pin C inside (to the left of) two pairs. Take one new pair of bobbins, place the thread under the weaver and bring it up so that it falls inside pin C and is supported by the weaver. Refer to figure 105.

Use the two outside pairs to work the footside stitch. Pin C is already in position, ignore the outer pair and work back across to the left using the other pair. Twist the weaver but do not work the footside stitch yet. Put up pin D, and introduce another pair. Take it under and up to fall to the right of pin D supported by the weaver. Now work the footside pin, remembering that the pin is already in position. Continue introducing new pairs at E and F. There are now twelve pairs of bobbins in use. From F, there will be one footside pair on the extreme left; work through the next five pairs in cloth stitch. Put up pin G between the last pairs worked (to the left of the weaver) and cover with cloth stitch. These are the weaver pairs, working to the right to H and to the left to J.

At pin K introduce a new pair, hanging it over the weaver as previously described. There is no footside pin and the weaver returns directly through the new pair and the other four passive pairs. The new pair is left out to work diagonally into the work at L; it is taken into the footside trail by the weaver but immediately released for the rose ground. A new pair is introduced at every pinhole on the inner edge on side X, figure 101, in readiness for the rose ground. No pairs are introduced into the work on side Z; they all enter diagonally from the lace having worked across from side X.

Care is necessary on side Z to have pairs available for the rose ground as follows. When a pair has been linked in and released at L, the weaver returns to the footside, works the stitch and travels back through the passive pairs. (In this position it lies as sixth pair from the right.) Take this pair, and the pair released from L, to work cloth stitch and twist without a pin in readiness for the rose ground unit. When the pairs from side X are available, the cloth stitch and twist is worked and the unit completed. It is very important to work the unit completely, including the final cloth stitches and twists. Only then can the sixth pair from the right work out to the edge as a weaver for the footside. On its return it works through and releases the other pair from the rose ground at pin M. Later the weaver which has been worked to N works with the pair from M for the rose ground unit. However work is always completed in diagonal rows and the rose ground unit near the side X must be worked first.

Two varieties of rose ground have been used, refer to A and D, and the illustrations on pages 59 and 60. Other varieties may be selected at the discretion of the lacemaker.

Flower centres

These are worked in half stitch. At the top pinhole work a half stitch, using the right-hand pair from the top left side leaf and the left-hand pair from the top right side leaf. Cover the pin with half stitch and work the diamond, keeping the same weaver throughout, bringing in two leaf pairs at each pin, and discarding two pairs for leaves after each pin for the lower leaves.

The corner

Refer to figure 103. When the edge pin G has been worked, bring the weaver to the right through two pairs only. It becomes a passive pair. Take the next pair to the right (lying fifth from the left) and work to the left through three pairs in cloth stitch; twist it twice, and work the corner pin H with the outside pair, as usual putting the pin inside (to the right of) two pairs. Bring the inner pair back through all four passive pairs. Now take the last pair passed through (the fifth from the left-hand side), and work to the left through three passive pairs in cloth stitch, twist it twice and work the outside stitch with the edge pair and put up pin J. As usual the outer pair is ignored, and the inner pair returns through the four passive pairs to the inside corner pin K which is used for a second time. The rearrangement of pairs in the corner makes a better edge and sharper corner.

The third side and the discarding of pairs

On this side, pairs are taken into the trail at each pin and later discarded. This has not been shown on the illustration, but is explained below. Refer to figure 103. The weaver works through one additional pair at M; pin M is put up and the weaver travels back to the footside. The pair taken in at M becomes a passive pair. To avoid increasing the number of passive pairs the third passive from the right-hand side is discarded. It is placed back across the work and cut off later. Similarly, at P a pair is taken in and, after pin Q has been worked, the third passive from the right is discarded. Continue to bring in and discard pairs all along this edge.

To complete

Refer to figure 106. Work as far as possible until all rose ground is complete. Work both sides to R. Work the weavers together with cloth stitch and twist, put up pin R between them and cover with cloth stitch. Take the left-hand pair and continue weaving to the footside at pin S. The other weaver becomes a passive pair and part of the combined trail. Continue to discard pairs to reduce the number, and work to pin X. Cross the outside pairs under the other threads and tie the bundle tightly. Cut off the threads which have been discarded close to the lace; they will remain in position and the cloth work will be close around them. Cut off the bobbins from the bundle and cut the ends short after the work has been removed from the pillow. The ends must be sewn in when the lace is attached to the fabric.

DAISY TRIANGLE

This pattern originates from Portugal. It is interesting to see another variation in rose ground, and this has been retained in the lace shown in figure 107. It is very similar to figure 63C. The centres of the daisies are very tight, and the footside has a combination of straight and twisted pairs. The pricking is given in figure 108. The same principle is used as in the previous triangle, however the scallop effect on the longest side will necessitate the addition of extra pairs on this side. These are carried as extra passive pairs when not required. Before starting, study figure 109. The rose ground units are shown in the usual way using small diamonds. The crosses show the arrangement of pairs between the units and as they approach the scallop edge.

Fig 107 *Daisy Triangle*

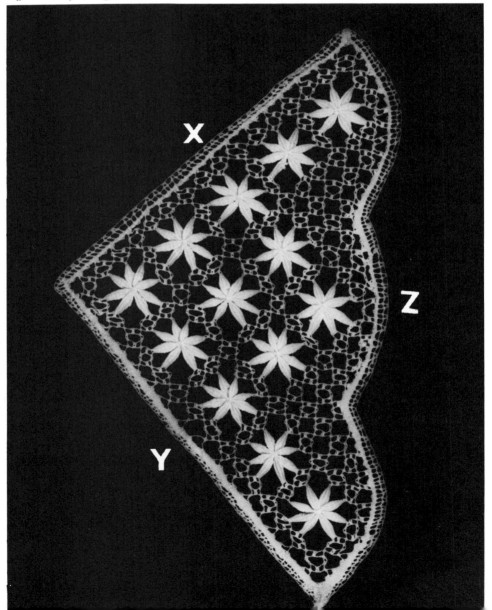

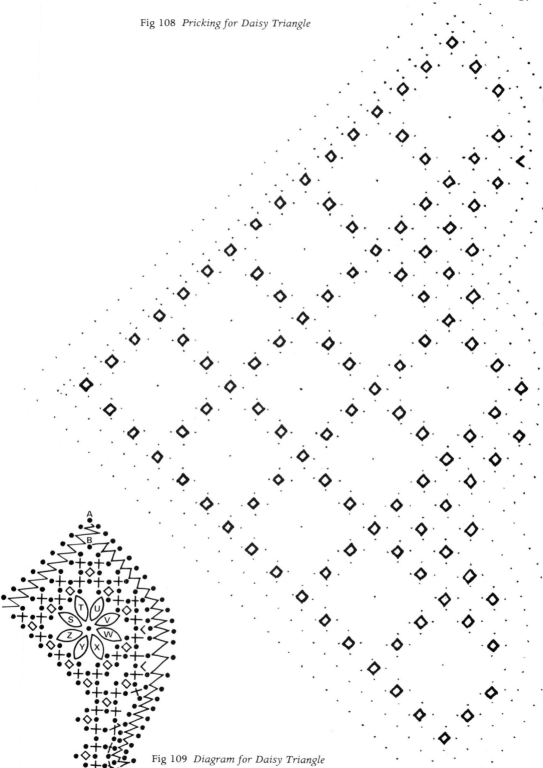

Fig 108 *Pricking for Daisy Triangle*

Fig 109 *Diagram for Daisy Triangle*

To begin

Hang twelve pairs round pin A. All pairs are joined in at this pin, it would be inconvenient to join in pairs when there is a twisted pair on the footside. Twist the left-hand two pairs at A twice each, and work them together in cloth stitch and twist. Ignore the outer pair and work through to the right-hand side with the other pair. Twist the weaver and the extreme right-hand pair twice each and work cloth stitch and twist. Put up the pin inside two pairs and work back with the inner of the two pairs. The trail is divided at B in the same way as in the previous pattern. The footside on the left-hand side of the triangle has a pair joined in at every pin as in the previous pattern. However the curved edge on the right side necessitates the joining in of one pair at each of the first six pinholes on the inner side of the trail. The seventh hole on this side has no pair entering or leaving the trail, but at the eighth hole one pair from the rose ground unit is linked into the trail, then immediately leaves it to work with its partner from the rose ground to make the side stitch of a part unit. This is neat, but the working diagram must be studied carefully to obtain the correct effect.

The rose ground

This is similar to that shown in figure 63C. Refer to figure 62. The stitches at a, b, g and h are given one extra twist. The stitch used before pins c, d, e and f is cloth stitch and twist, but after the pins it is cloth stitch and two twists on each pair.

The centre of the daisy: first method

Work the four leaves S, T, U and V. Take the four threads of leaf U and pass them to the right over the first pair and under the second pair of leaf V. Take the four threads of leaf T, and pass them to the left under the first pair and over the second pair of leaf S. The four pairs from leaves S and V are in the centre. Using each pair as a single thread, work a half stitch and put up a centre pin, then pass the second pair of the four over the third pair to cover the pin.

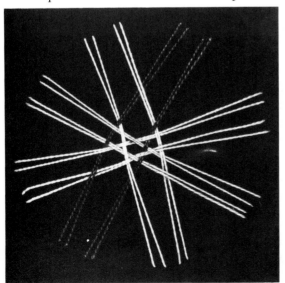

Take the four left hand threads over and under the next two pairs to bring them back to centre. Take the four right-hand threads under and over two pairs to the centre. Work leaves W and Z and then leaves X and Y. In order to achieve a close centre the leaves must be exactly the correct length and worked in the order stated.

The centre of the daisy: second method

This is the more usual method, but it has the disadvantage of requiring more stitches, and therefore gives a less attractive centre. Refer to figure 110.

Fig 110 *Working the centre of the daisy*

Use the four plaits as eight pairs, using each pair as if it were a single bobbin.
Use the centre four pairs to make a half stitch. Make: a half stitch with the right-hand four pairs; a half stitch with the left-hand four pairs; a half stitch with the centre four pairs; a half stitch with the right-hand four pairs; and a half stitch with the left-hand four pairs.

Put up a pin in the centre, then make a cloth stitch with the centre four pairs. Find the right-hand four pairs, and cross the centre pairs left over right. Then find the left-hand four pairs, and cross the centre pairs left over right.

THE EXTENDED CORNER
To add interest or importance to a simple edging it may be extended in the corner. See figure 111. As the edging has a footside which has been worked out down a vertical line on graph paper, the footside across the corner will lie diagonally across the squares. Figure 112 shows the edging.

Fig 111 *Extended Corner pattern*

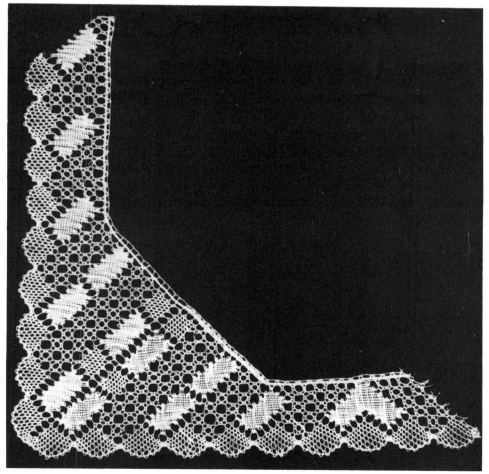

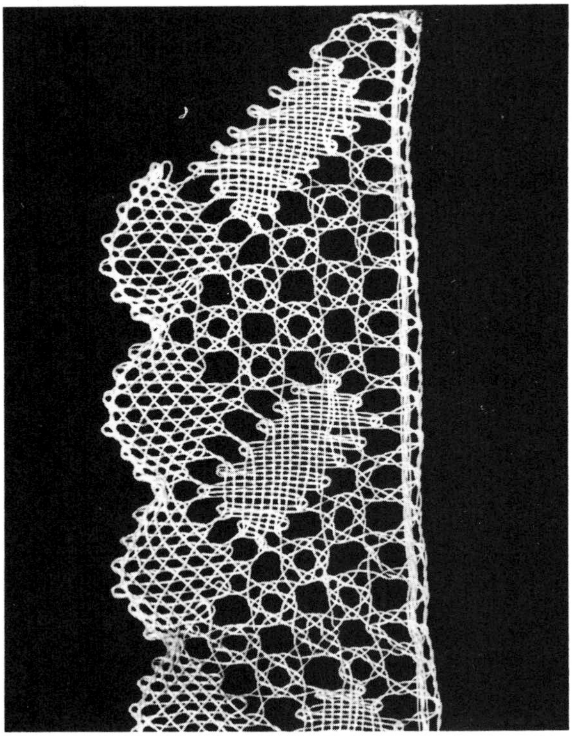

Fig 112 *The edging of the extended corner*

To work the corner

Refer to figure 113. Pairs are joined in at every pinhole from A to B. In the previous patterns the pairs were added on the inner edge of the footside trail, but in this pattern it is not feasible as the pairs are needed to work the row of pins next to the footside as part of rose ground units or cloth rectangles. In order to provide the pairs needed for the left-hand side of the rose ground unit, work as follows.

Use the footside weaver from O as the first pair. Put up pin A between the threads of the extreme right-hand pair, hang one pair round pin A to fall inside these threads, twist the two threads on each side of the pin three times each. The threads to the left of the pin weave through the passive pairs to become the second pair for the rose ground, a, and the threads to the right of the pin remain in that position as the edge pair. Repeat this method at every pinhole as far as and including pin B.

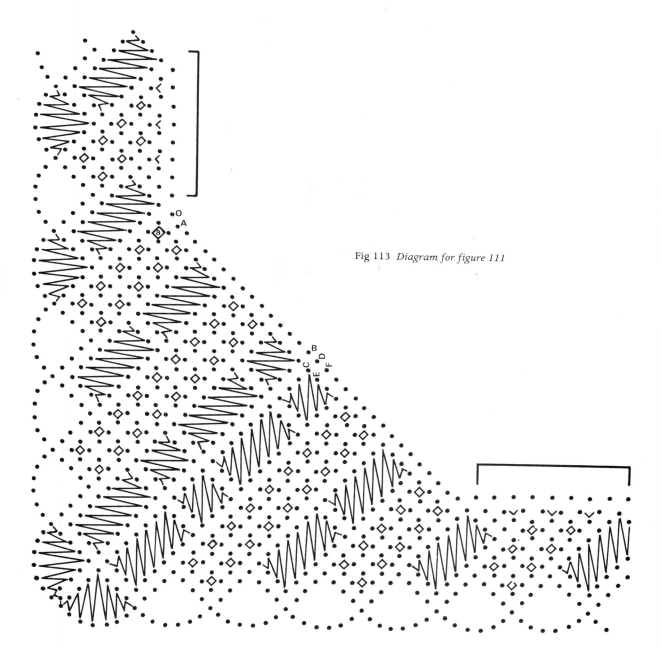

Fig 113 *Diagram for figure 111*

The pattern should be worked completely to the corner diagonal and the extra pin between the fans on the headside worked too. Turn the pillow. When the rectangles and diamonds have been worked proceed as follows. Take the pair from C and work the footside and pin D. Ignore the outer pair as usual, and bring the inner pair back through one passive pair only. Take the pair from E and work to F. Continue and discard unwanted pairs in the footside trail.

A reversal of the pattern will be necessary. Refer to the photograph and figure 114.

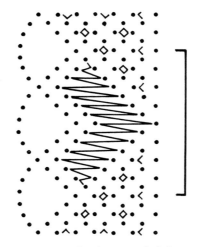

Fig 114 *Diagram for the reversal of the pattern*

8 – Circular Edgings and Collars

CIRCULAR EDGINGS

In order to plan a pattern as an edging for a circle it is necessary to make a grid on which to work. Normal graph paper is suitable for lace with a straight footside, but a polar or circular graph may be used when making the pricking for an edging on a curve. Collars may be worked out on the same graphs, but as they are not intended for making lace patterns, one must decide how to use the lines available to best advantage. Refer to the polar graph on page 151 and work as follows.

(1) Mark in the radii to isolate the section, in this case one quarter of the circle. It is usual to plan patterns for either one third, one quarter, or one sixth of the circle, and then reprick to achieve the complete edging.

(2) Select a circular line for the footside and prick a hole at every radial intersection.

(3) Select the concentric line that is the same distance from the footside as the distance apart of the footside holes, and prick in radial intersections. In this case, a line three spaces from the footside was used.

(4) Continue to prick in radial intersections on further concentric lines that are equidistant from each other. The result is a square formation of holes. Refer to grid I on page 153. This cannot be used for the usual type of Torchon pattern, but it was used successfully for the collar in figure 123.

(5) Prick in holes diagonally between existing holes to achieve grid J on page 154.

These grids have disadvantages and a limited use. As the work is planned in concentric circles, the holes towards the perimeter become increasingly further apart. As the concentric lines are equidistant, the angle of working becomes more acute. On the whole these grids are suitable only for narrow prickings. Figure 115 gives the circular pricking for lace in figure 20. The number of footside holes in one repeat of pattern must be divisible into the total number of footside holes in the circle. The grid explained above has 180 holes and the pattern only four.

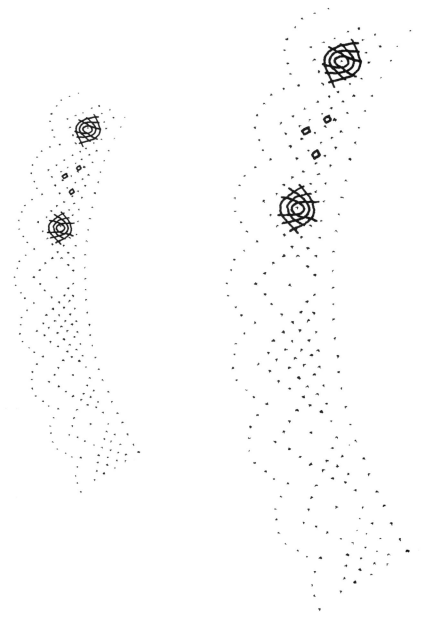

Fig 115 *Circular pricking for Spanish Torchon pattern (figure 20)*

Therefore 45 repeats are possible. As alternating rose ground and spider would necessitate two similar repeats adjacent to each other, it is essential that the pattern be adapted and thought of in groups of three. Half stitch fills in the increased area of the headside adequately.

Figure 115 gives the circular pricking for lace in figure 82. The tallies are used

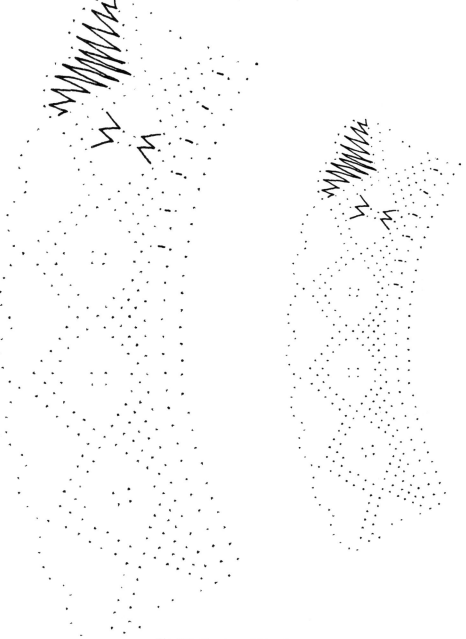

Fig 116 *Circular pricking for Heart and Spider pattern (figure 82)*

to extend the width, and this may be applied to any pattern. Grid L on page 155 has been prepared with tallies and used for this pricking. As there are six holes on the footside in each repeat, it will fit into the circular grid satisfactorily. Although the pattern is wider, it looks attractive as the spider is open, and fits into the pricking when spread out towards the head.

Any pattern may be designed on a circular grid provided that the following points are remembered.

(1) The footside holes for each repeat should fit into the total circle.
(2) The pattern is narrow to avoid distortion on the outside edge.
(3) Suitable stitches and features are used to 'fill' and disguise the outer edge.

Figure 117 gives another pattern possibility. Half stitch is particularly successful on the headside, other possibilities are suggested in the next patterns. Figure 118 is similar to the lace in figure 25, but the trail is in cloth and the diamond in half stitch. Also extra pinholes are put in the scallop to improve the larger curve. Figure 119 is similar to the lace in figure 165 but each pattern repeat has been reduced by one pinhole. The fan is worked in cloth stitch and twist to fill the curve.

DIAMOND PATTERN

If a wider pattern is required it is necessary to rearrange the holes and make a complete break in the centre. Refer to grid M on page 155. The inner section was worked out as for grid J. Two trails of passives with tallies make the break before the outer section is arranged with the holes nearer together. In order to plan the outer section, prick holes for the tallies to correspond with alternate pins on the inner section. To reduce the distance between holes on the ever increasing curve, prick two holes equidistant between these. If this line of holes is repeated on concentric circles as before, the square formation will be achieved. The holes diagonally between can be put in 'by eye'. Figure 120 gives a pattern using this grid. Six repeats are necessary for a full circle. The outside edge is worked as in figure 121. Work in letter order; L, B and M link with the half stitch ground to the right of the line on the pricking – this line denotes two pairs of threads. The edging may be used alone as a narrow pattern. The lace is shown in the frontispiece (on the title page) and figure 122.

COLLARS

As Torchon lace relies on a geometric arrangement of threads and stitches, the designing of collars has severe limitations. As already explained, the pattern becomes distorted towards the outside edge; furthermore the uneven curve of the neckline will require modification to achieve a satisfactory pricking. The lacemaker who wants more freedom should work collars of Beds-Maltese lace. In order to make a collar to fit a specific garment, it is essential to use a pattern of the correct size. Hours of work may be followed by disappointment when the finished collar does not fit the garment for which it is intended. It is advisable to take a rubbing from the pricking, cut it out and place it in position on the garment.

When designing a collar, it is necessary to have an exact copy of the neck edge. This may be made directly from the garment or from a commercial pattern. If using the paper pattern, trim away the seam allowance at the neck edge, the

Fig 117 *Circular pricking for a spider and rose ground pattern*

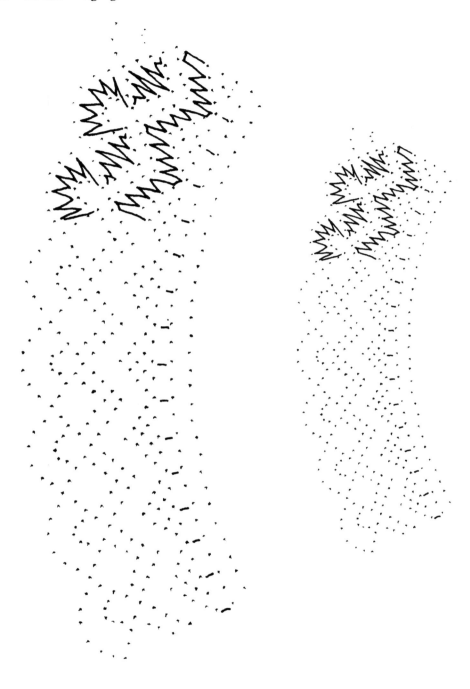

Fig 118 *Circular pricking for a trail and diamond pattern*

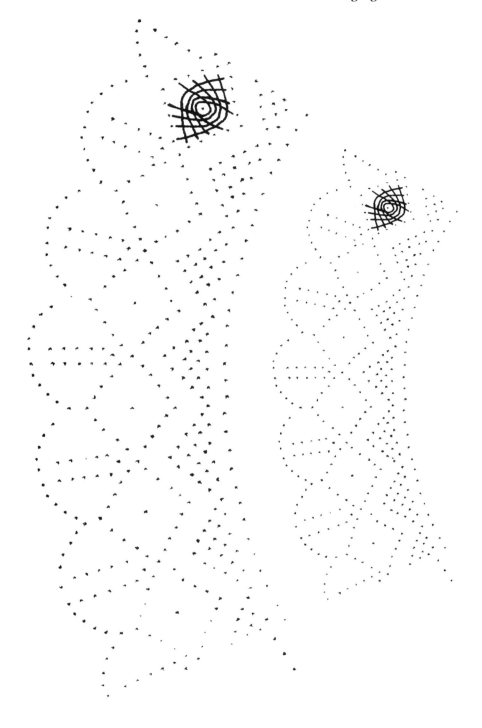

Fig 119 *Circular pricking for a rose ground and daisy pattern*

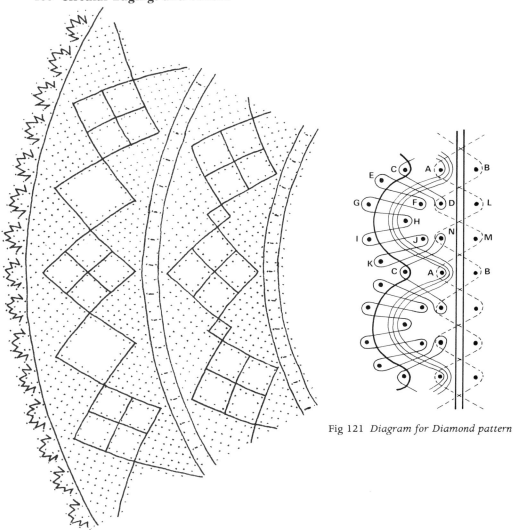

Fig 121 *Diagram for Diamond pattern*

Fig 120 *Circular pricking for Diamond pattern*

centre front and centre back of the bodice pieces. Fasten the front and back together at the shoulder, matching the stitching line and balance marks if any. Lay this over strong paper and mark the neck curve and the centre front and back lines. The collar pattern supplied is unsuitable unless it lies flat upon the garment. If using the garment to make the outline, place it over the corner of a table or an ironing board, and similarly mark in the neck outline. Estimate the width of the collar required and draw in a second curve.

If the garment fastens at the centre back, two-piece collars are more suitable. Collars made in one piece are suitable only for a garment with a centre front opening. Some lacemakers are deterred at the thought of making a collar in two pieces, but the advantages are numerous. It may be eased to fit the neck edge more

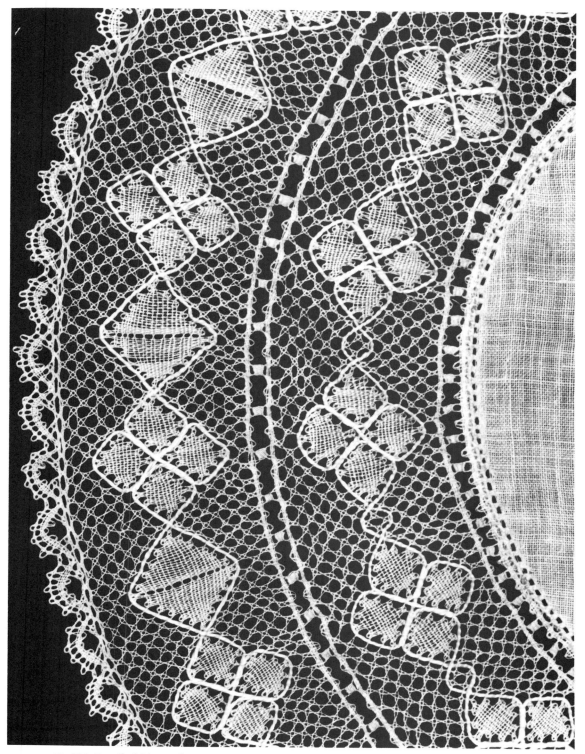

Fig 122 *Detail of Diamond pattern*

readily, also the centre front edges can be worked in exactly the same way to achieve a perfect match. Although it is possible to work a neat and apparently similar beginning and ending to a piece of lace, it is impossible to have an identical arrangement of threads. A collar in one piece will rarely fit onto a normal pillow, and much care and time is taken to move the lace as it is worked. The three collars described below are worked in two pieces and will fit onto an average size pillow.

When making collars for children, they can be made larger than required to allow for attachment to larger garments later. The neck edge, which is the footside, may be gathered slightly, or alternatively a narrow braid may be worked separately and the collar attached to this, with the added advantage that when the lace and braid are removed from the garment the lace is undamaged and, if necessary, the braid can be replaced. Collars for adults may be adjusted in the same way, or for permanent reduction in size the braid may be incorporated as part of the actual collar pattern. Instructions for this alteration are included with the instructions for the second collar.

To design the Torchon collar, cut out the collar shape and place it on a piece of circular graph paper. Refer to the grid on page 151. Move the collar shape until the neck edge corresponds (imperfectly) with a circular line on the graph paper. The collar shape must be transferred onto the graph paper and the neck edge adjusted to match one of the lines. The method for arranging the holes is the same as for the circular edgings. Three collars, each using a different arrangement of holes, are included but students are advised to plan their own.

SQUARE-MESH COLLAR
Refer to figures 123 and 124. The arrangement is less usual as the pinholes are placed where radial and concentric lines intersect each other. Grid I on page 153 is arranged in this manner. With experience, the lacemaker will learn to select a mesh of size suitable for the threads to be used. The weaver will follow the radial lines across the collar and the other threads will fall parallel to the neck edge. Normally Torchon patterns are based on a diagonal line of working, and the square mesh method imposes severe limitations upon the design which is reduced to tallies and rectangular blocks. However, pleasing effects may be obtained and the lace is quick to make. This type of lace requires a very firm edge; notice how the weaver has been used to form cloth blocks and the passive pairs have been twisted to avoid loose cloth where the holes are further apart.

To work the collar
Prepare the pricking, and refer to figures 125 and 126. Nineteen pairs of bobbins will be required. Suitable threads are the Swedish linen no. 50 or DMC pearl cotton no. 12. Hang two pairs on A, B and F and one pair on each of C, D, E and G. Twist the two threads to the right of pins A, B and F twice each. Using the right hand pair from A, work in cloth stitch to the right through the seven pairs from B, C, D, E and F. Work the pair from G to the right through the first pair in cloth

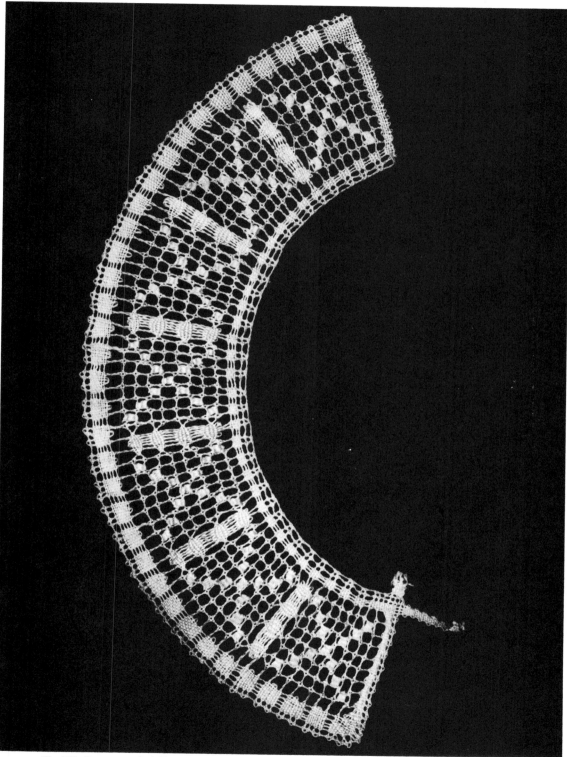

Fig 123 *Square-mesh Collar*

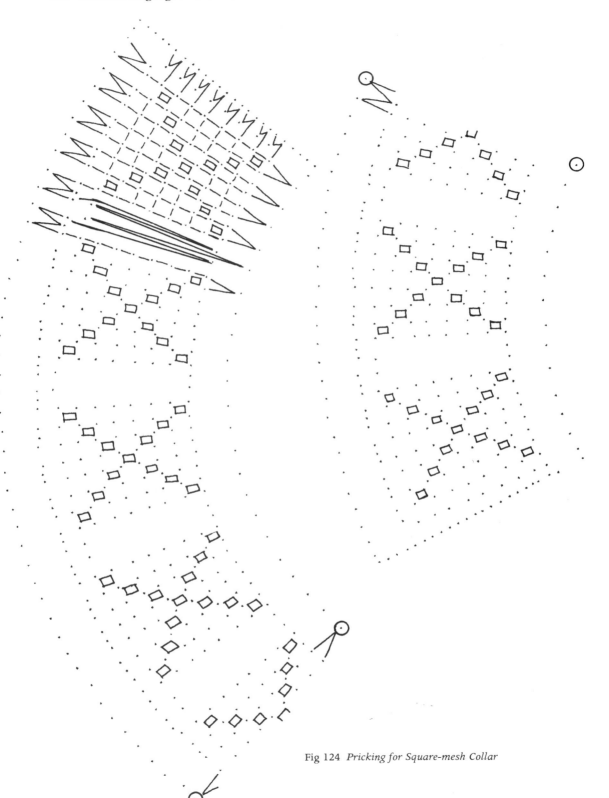

Fig 124 *Pricking for Square-mesh Collar*

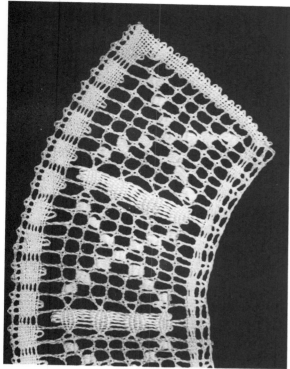

Fig 125 *Beginning the collar*

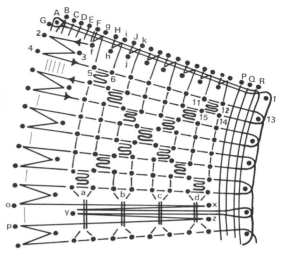

Fig 126 *Diagram for figure 125*

stitch and twist and through the other seven pairs in cloth stitch.

Put up pin f between the pairs hanging from F and cover it with cloth stitch and twist. Work the right-hand pair in cloth stitch through two pairs to the right. Twist the weaver twice and put up pin g, weave back through two pairs and leave the pair hanging in readiness for pin 5. Hang one pair on pin H and work through two pairs to the left in cloth stitch, twist the weaver twice and put up pin h. Weave back in cloth stitch, twist the weaver twice and put up pin i. Weave to the left through the same two pairs and leave hanging in readiness for pin 6. Hang one pair on J and repeat the method using pins j and k.

Continue across the work, hanging on pairs as required until a pair hangs in readiness for pin 12. Hang one pair on each of pins at P, Q and R; work the two passive pairs hanging horizontally across the top through these pairs and then work the passive pairs together in cloth stitch and twist. Put up pin 1 between these two pairs. The pair hanging from pin f is the weaver and works cloth stitch five times to the left, twist the weaver once and work cloth stitch and twist with the outside pair. Put up pin 2, twist the weaver once more and work back to pin 3 through the same pairs with the same sequence of stitches (ie cloth stitch and twist and five cloth stitches).

Work to pins 4 and 5. Before working pin 5 twist both pairs (ie the weaver and the pair from g) twice each. Make a half stitch, put up pin 5 and cover with half stitch and one extra twist. Give the pair hanging from i two twists and work half stitch with this pair and the right-hand pair from 5. Put up pin 6 and cover with half stitch and an extra twist. Continue until pin 12 is complete, weave on through the pairs from P, Q and R in cloth stitch, twist the weaver once, and work cloth stitch and twist through the last two pairs. Pin inside two pairs as usual, ignore the outer pair and work back through with cloth stitch and twist and three cloth stitches.

Pairs from 11 and 12 make a tally and are used for pins 14 and 15 as in the previous row. Pairs from 5 and 6 make a tally similarly. On the left (the headside) the outer passive pair requires one extra twist and the other five passive pairs two twists on each to give the cloth stitch block effect. Complete the pattern to o. Work pairs together in cloth stitch at a, b, c and d; there are no pins at these points.

Weave from o through the edging as usual and through pairs from a in cloth stitch. Twist the weaver three times and work through the pairs from b in cloth stitch. Continue through pairs from c and d and put up pin x. Return to pin y and all the way back to the footside pin. Weave back using pin y a second time and then to pin z. Weave to pin p. Arrange the threads attractively in the cloth and bring the pairs together to correspond with points a, b, c and d. Work cloth stitch and two twists with the pairs; there are no pins. Continue.

Fig 127 *Completing the collar*

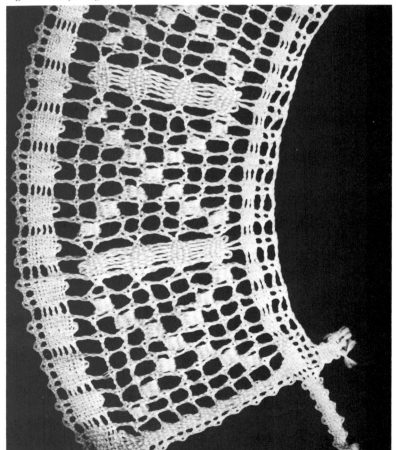

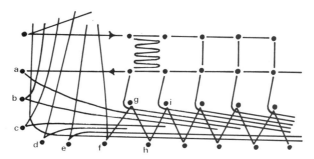

Fig 128 *Diagram for figure 127*

To complete the collar

Refer to figures 127 and 128. Work the last pattern as far as pin a and weave back through six passive pairs. Take the second pair from the left and work to the edge in cloth stitch and twist. Put up pin b and cover with cloth stitch and twist. Work to the right through the remaining four passive pairs in cloth stitch. Repeat to work pin c, cover and back through three passive pairs. Repeat to work pin d, cover and back through two pairs and then pin e, cover and back through the one remaining pair. Take the last passive pair to work pin f. Give the pillow a half turn to the left and take the weaver from f through the edge pairs in cloth stitch and twist and through the five pairs hanging at the corner. Continue through one more pair hanging from the tally. Put up pin g. Discard the third pair from the left by placing it back over the work. Continue to weave to h and i and discard a pair as before.

Continue similarly across the end of the collar. In the corner, weave the footside pairs through the edge pairs and continue to weave a short tape. Discard pairs to achieve a neat even finish. The pairs from the edge are woven into a short tape and then knotted firmly; they are folded across the footside, and the extended footside tape is sewn back across these ends and the footside.

Rub the pricking to get the pattern reversed for the second half of the collar. It will be worked with the footside on the left in order to work from front to back.

DIAMOND AND ROSE GROUND COLLAR

Refer to figures 129 and 130. This is a typical Torchon design and was planned using the grid on page 154. A cloth stitch edging is used for easy laundering and to contrast with the half stitch diamonds and rose ground. Because distortion occurs this is suitable for a narrow collar only. When the outline has been established, mark in the ground holes inside the collar shape. As far as possible place the holes on the inner edge of the cloth edge in sequence with the other holes in the design. The outer holes may be put in on an even curve 'by eye' later. Consideration should be given to centre front and back, and the holes for the curve should be plotted in close relation to the holes within the pattern, in order to achieve an attractive design.

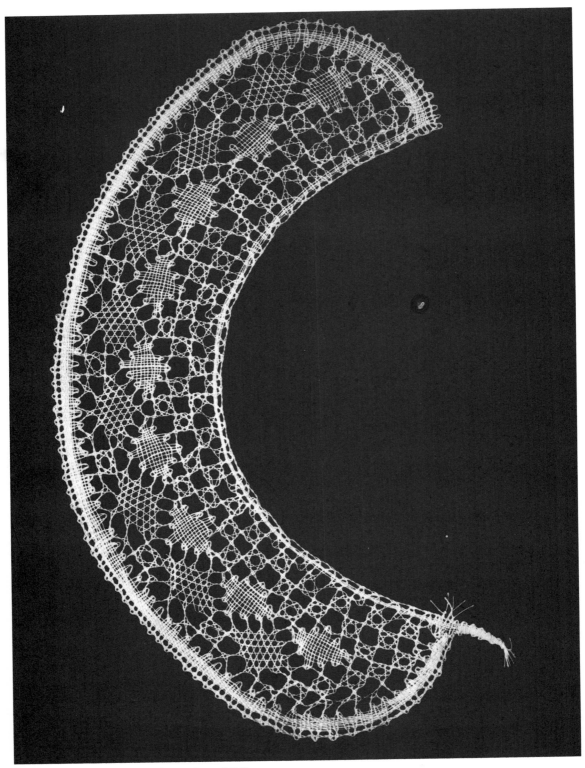

Fig 129 *Diamond and Rose Ground Collar*

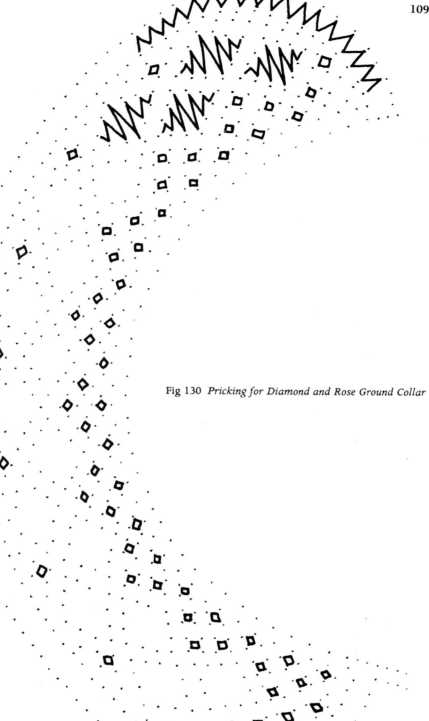

Fig 130 *Pricking for Diamond and Rose Ground Collar*

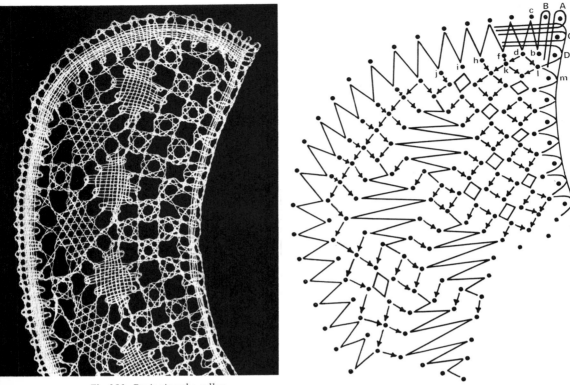

Fig 131 *Beginning the collar*

Fig 132 *Diagram for figure 131*

To work the collar

Prepare the pricking, and refer to figures 131 and 132. For the thread, Swedish linen no. 60 or Fils à Dentelles no. 70 (DMC) is recommended. Hang two pairs on each of A and B and twist the threads to the right of each pin twice each. Hang two pairs on C and take the left hand two threads to the left through the four pairs hanging from A and B in cloth stitch, and twist. The pairs from A are now worked together in cloth stitch. The left hand pair works cloth stitch through two pairs to the left. To begin the footside, hang two pairs on pin C. There are four threads to the right of pin C, twist each pair twice and work cloth stitch and twist. This is a method of retaining the straight footside when joining in new pairs; refer to figure 133. Put up pin D to the left of one pair and join in two new pairs as at pin C. Take the left-hand pair from C through three pairs to the left in cloth stitch; take the right-hand pair through the same three pairs. Take the left-hand pair from D through similarly. There are one twisted and four straight pairs along the 'top' edge, these are the pairs for the curved edge of the collar.

To establish the footside, take the pair to the right of pin D and work to the left through two pairs in cloth stitch. These are passive pairs which remain on the footside (neck edge) throughout.

Continue with the curved edge of the collar using the fifth pair from the right;

Fig 133 *Retaining the straight footside when joining in new pairs*

this pair was originally to the left of B. Put up pin b to the left of this pair and work to the left through the five pairs keeping the correct pattern. (Cloth stitch four times, twist the weaver and then cloth stitch and twist.) Put up pin c to the right of the weaver and work back to d. Join in two new pairs at d, one pair at f and one pair at h. Continue to join in pairs as required.

The left-hand pair from d and the pair from f work a half stitch, then pin k is put up and covered with half stitch. Two pairs from i, and one pair from each of j, and the diagonal row from k will make the first rose ground unit. As pin i is part of the unit the preliminary stitches cannot be worked, however they must be worked after the four pins are in position. The footside weaver from D and the right hand pair from d make a half stitch; pin l is put up and covered with half stitch. The footside and pin m is worked, and the pair is available for the rose ground. The ground is worked to the cloth diamond. Join in pairs as required and continue to work the collar.

To complete the collar
Pairs are discarded gradually in the cloth of the curved edge; refer to figure 134. As pairs are brought in from the rose ground and become part of the cloth edging, the third pair from the left is discarded regularly to prevent unsightly thickness. The work is finished as for the first collar, and neatened.

To reduce the length of the neck curve
Refer to figure 135 for the method of working. Hang two pairs on A and twist the two right hand threads twice. Place two pairs round a pin at C and work as in

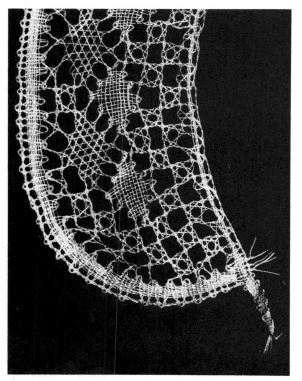

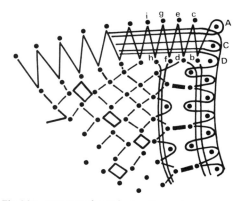

Fig 134 *Completing the collar*

Fig 135 *Diagram for reducing the neck curve*

Fig 136 *Scalloped Collar*

figure 132 and the accompanying instructions. Work the pairs from A together in cloth stitch and join in two pairs at each of C and D as in the above pattern. The left-hand pair from A becomes the first straight passive as in the previous pattern, but the right-hand pair becomes the weaver for the outer curved edge. Work this pair through two pairs from C and one pair from D in cloth stitch. Introduce one new pair at b, this will be the right-hand footside passive. Weave back to c, keeping one twisted pair on the outside edge. Continue introducing new pairs as required. Two pairs at d are needed to supply the second footside passive pair and the weaver for the inner trail. Pairs from f and h provide the passives for the inner trail.

SCALLOPED COLLAR

A wider collar may be planned, but a break in the centre is essential to avoid distortion. Grid M on page 155 may be used, and the method is the same as for the pricking in figure 120. The collar is shown in figure 136.

To work the collar

Refer to figures 137 and 138. Use figure 139 to make the pricking. The working diagram clarifies the method of starting, this is similar to the previous collar. As the outer edge is worked in half stitch, this necessitates a different method for

Fig 137 *Beginning the collar*

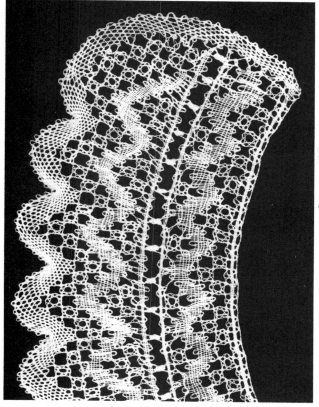

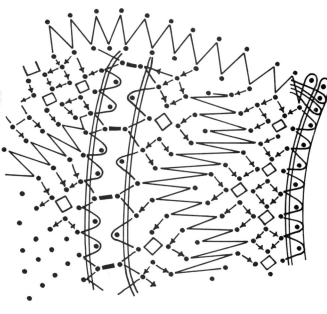

Fig 138 *Diagram for figure 137*

Fig 139 *Pricking for Scalloped Collar*

completion, as pairs cannot be discarded satisfactorily in half stitch. The second pair from the edge is discarded, knotted very firmly, and cut off. As the side of the lace nearer the worker is the wrong side, the knots are underneath and unnoticed. The footside pairs are brought into the half stitch (refer to figure 140) and the edge completed in cloth stitch.

Fig 140 *Completing the collar*

9 – Patterns with Plaits and Picots

Plaits and picots are associated with Bedfordshire-Maltese lace. Frequently these features are combined with the geometric arrangement of holes found in Torchon patterns, and a knowledge of their execution will add interest and variety.

THE PLAIT
See figure 141. The plait consists of two pairs of bobbins worked continuously in half stitch. In order to achieve good tension the pairs are pulled well to the sides between each stitch.

THE PICOT
Refer to figure 142. Take the two left-hand threads of the plait in the left hand, and hold them taut. Take a pin in the right hand, put it under the right of these two threads, and pull the left thread across under the right thread (142A) so that the

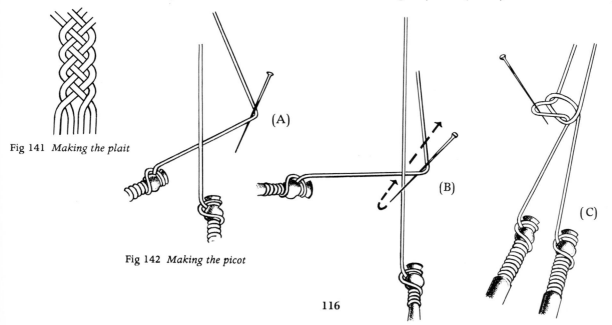

Fig 141 *Making the plait*

(A)

(B)

(C)

Fig 142 *Making the picot*

threads are crossed. Bring the pin towards the worker over the crossed threads, then turn the point of the pin away, taking it under the crossed threads and up between them (142B). Stick the pin into the picot hole, usually to the left of the plait, and ease the threads until a single picot thread appears about the pin (142C). If the lacemaker is accustomed to using double picots with fine thread, these may be used.

THE CROSSING OF PLAITS

Four-plait crossing

To work the four-plait crossing, use the two plaits and consider them as four pairs, using each pair as a single bobbin as in cloth stitch. Place the second over the third. At the same time take the fourth over the third and the second over the first. Put up a pin in the centre. Place the second over the third. Figure 143 shows the complete crossing.

Six-plait crossing

To work a six-plait crossing, use the three plaits and consider each pair as a single thread. Spread the pairs out on the pillow for easy identification, keeping each pair close together. Take the right centre pair over the next pair to the right. Take the left centre pair under the next pair to the left. Cross the new centre pairs right over left, then put up a pin between them. Take the pair to the right of the pin out to the right over the next pair and under the outside pair. Take the pair to the left of the pin out to the left under the next pair and over the outside pair. Find the new centre pairs and take the right pair over the next pair to the right. Take the left centre pair under the next pair to the left. Cross the new centre pairs right over left. Take the right centre pair over the next pair to the right, and the left centre pair under the next pair to the left. Figure 144 shows the completed crossing.

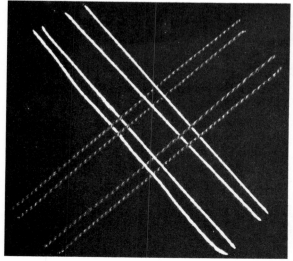

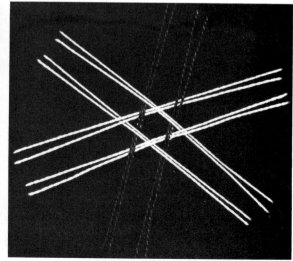

Fig 143 *Four-plait crossing*

Fig 144 *Six-plait crossing*

Fig 145 *Square Plaits patterns*

SQUARE PLAITS PATTERN

Refer to figures 145, 146 and 147. Holes for picots have been omitted from the diagram, but should be positioned on the pricking as in the photograph.

To begin

Hang two pairs on pin A, twist the right-hand pair and cover with cloth stitch and twist. Hang up a pair on a support pin behind the work, and work through it in cloth stitch and twist with the left-hand pair from A. This is the twisted passive

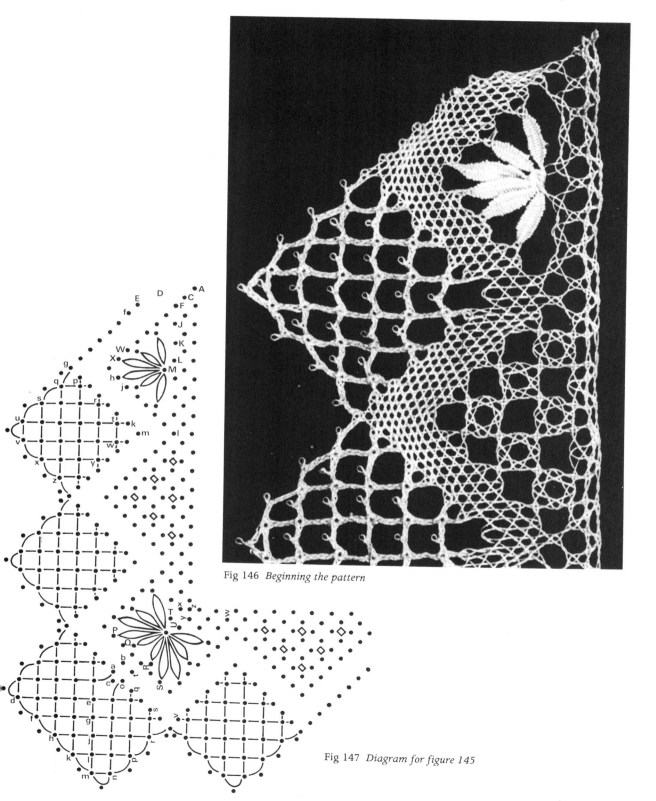

Fig 146 *Beginning the pattern*

Fig 147 *Diagram for figure 145*

pair. Hang another pair on a support pin and work the first ground stitch (half stitch, put up pin C, and cover with half stitch). The right-hand pair at C returns to work the footside, and the left-hand pair waits to become part of the half stitch trail.

Hang one pair on a pin at E, and three pairs on a support pin behind the work at D. The pair at E is weaver and works in half stitch through the three pairs on D and the left hand pair at C. Pin F is put up to the left of the weaver; the weaver travels to the right through the trail pairs in half stitch. Two pairs are introduced at every pinhole on the left side of the trail from f to g inclusive. Remember to leave out one pair at pins F to W inclusive, and two pairs at X.

The leaves and footside

Work the footside and ground to L. Note that the pair at J which should work to the left in this pattern drops vertically to work ground pin K. Similarly L is worked with the left-hand pair from K. Three leaves are worked. The first leaf uses pairs from two trail pins and these are brought together with half stitch, pin, half stitch before commencing the leaf. The second leaf is started in the same way, but the third leaf uses two pairs directly from the trail. These three leaves make a six-plait crossing as described above at M. However it is necessary to link in the pair from pin L. Work as follows. Work the crossing as far as the pin, put up the pin. Take the pair from L to the left and pass it under the three pairs that are to the right of the pin, take it behind the pin and bring it back over the same three pairs. Complete the crossing. Work the footside to have all pairs available for the trail.

The trail

Find the weaver for the trail at g, and work as far as m. Leave out two pairs after every pin from g to k inclusive. Two pairs will be brought in at h and one pair at every pin from j to l inclusive. Extra care is necessary when leaving out pairs for plaits to ensure that the weaver remains the same throughout.

The plaits

In this pattern picots are used only on vertical plaits. Work the small plaits and the crossing at p. Work the two plaits from p, then work the plait and picot from g, and work the crossing at q. Work the plaits from q. Work pin r and the plaits and crossings across the pattern to s. Work from t to u. Having made the picot on the outside point, work from v to w, x to y and z.

The trail

Return to the trail and the weaver at m, and take in the pairs from the plait. Continue with the trail, taking in two plait pairs at every pin on the left, and leaving out one pair at every pin on the right.

Rose ground

Work the rose ground and continue.

The corner
Notice that the trail is completed before the corner diagonal and restarted afterwards, as in the pattern in figures 25 and 165.

The ground
Work the ground to pin T. Work the corner pin z using a pair from x.

The leaves
Three leaves are made as usual, and the six-plait crossing completed introducing the pair from T. Two leaves are made to P and Q, and the remaining two pairs wait at the centre; no leaf is worked.

The trail
The trail is worked completely to a. Two pairs are left out after every pin on the left side; on the right, two pairs are taken in at P and one at each of the other two pins. One pair will be left out after b, and three pairs left at a will be required, two for the plait and the other for the trail when the corner has been turned.

The plaits
Work normally to pin d. At pin c there is no plait available for a crossing and the pin is put in the centre of the plait pairs, both pairs are twisted, and the plait is continued to the left. From pin d the plait is worked to the right as far as possible, and a crossing worked at e. The crossing is worked at f, and the plaiting taken to g. Similarly pins h to j, k, l and m are worked.

Turn the pillow ready to work the next side. From n work to c. Hook two of the plait pairs through the plait at c. To facilitate this, remove the pin. Pass the other two threads through the loops and tie one knot. Replace the pin and plait to o. Work from p to q, r and s.

The trail
Use the two pairs from the plait from c and the pair from pin a. Work the pair from a to the left in half stitch through the pairs from the plait, then put up pin o. Weave back to the right to t, bringing in one pair from b. Continue, and on the left bring in two pairs at every pin. On the right a pair will be brought in from the previous trail at the corner pin. One pair is left out at the same pin and one pair at the next pin for the leaf R. Two pairs are left out at S and the trail is worked to v.

The leaves
Leaves are made from R and S to the centre. The centre pin is removed and the four pairs from the two leaves and the two pairs hanging in the centre make another six-plait crossing using the same pinhole. Pin U is worked using the pair that was linked into the plait crossing and the pair from T. Pin y is worked with a pair from U and a pair from z and the ground can be completed to w. Work the three leaves. The corner is complete and the edging may be continued, beginning with the trail.

CLOTH TRAIL AND NINEPIN EDGE PATTERN

The ninepin edge is typical of many Bedfordshire patterns. The number of pairs in the cloth depends on the thickness of the thread used, and a thread suitable for the Torchon ground must be selected. Detailed written instruction is unnecessary as figures 148 and 149 clarify the methods used. However, the following guidelines will be found helpful.

Fig 148 *Cloth Trail and Ninepin Edge pattern*

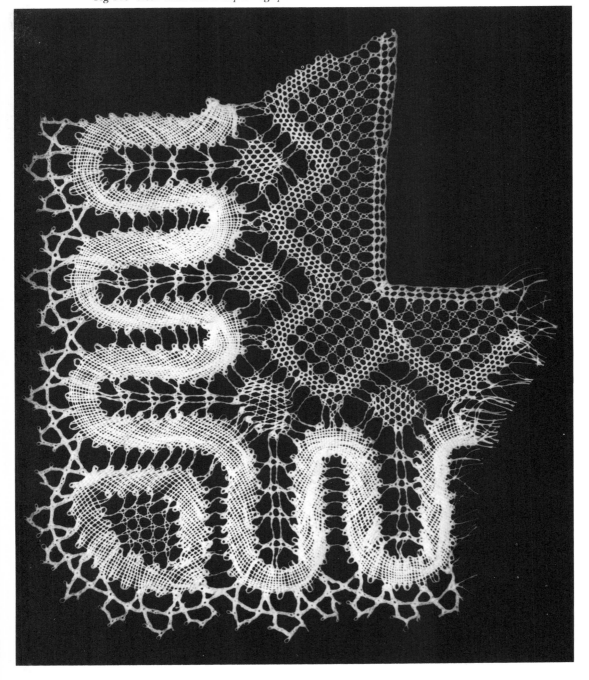

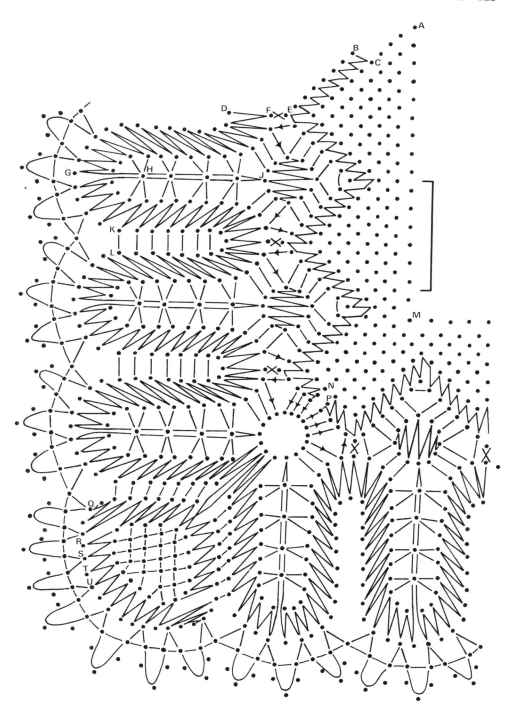

Fig 149 *Diagram for figure 148*

(1) Begin at pin A and work the footside pin and three ground stitches.

(2) Hang a weaver on B and work to the right through two pairs on support pins and through the pair waiting to enter from the trail. Put up pin C and work back across the half stitch trail. Bring in one pair at every pin on the left and leave out one pair at every pin on the right, wait at E.

(3) Hang one pair on the pin at D and nine pairs on a support pin to the right of D. Weave with the pair from D in cloth through the nine pairs, and put up the pin at F. Give the pairs at E and F an extra twist, and work cloth stitch and twist. Each pair is then given an extra twist; they have now changed position, and continue as weaver pairs on opposite trails. Apart from the ninepin edge there are no plaits in the pattern, and lines indicate pairs; with the exception of the half stitch ground all pairs are twisted at least twice.

(4) Note the half stitch trail arrangement as shown also on page 36.

(5) At G the trail weaver travels through to the half stitch diamond. At H work as follows. Bring the two pairs from the cloth together with cloth stitch and twist, and put up a pin in the centre between the pairs to support the stitch. Bring the weaver through with cloth stitch and twist. Now take the pins out and replace them, supporting the weaver as well as the pairs. Pin J is worked using the weaver, and the weaver from the diamond. The weaver returns to the cloth trail, passing through the pairs with cloth stitch and twist. Continue weaving the cloth trail to keep the tension firm. Take the pairs at H, and work cloth stitch and twist, then work the other pairs in the same way.

(6) Pairs will be left out at K and at the other pins on that edge. They will be well twisted and brought in when the trail comes back alongside, as at L.

(7) The corner footside pin M is worked at the beginning of the ground row to N. When the half stitch circle has been worked the pillow is turned and the ground row from P worked down to the corner, then pin M is used a second time.

(8) Six pairs are joined in at pin Q, a weaver and five passive pairs. The trail is split in the same way as in the triangular insertions and additional pairs are put in at R, S, T and U. This is explained on page 83. The pairs are left out to work half stitch, pin, half stitch ground in the centre of the cloth in the corner. Towards the end of the cloth stitch pairs will be thrown out, and the last few pairs should be plaited out with the ninepin edge plait and then discarded.

OPENING FLOWER PATTERN

This is an unusual pattern as the ground stitches are arranged in semicircles. The broad footside with tallies can be added to any pattern to increase the width or add interest. Refer to figure 150 and 151. Pricking 152 will give a larger piece of lace than will a pricking made from the working diagram.

To begin

Hang two pairs on A, twist the right-hand threads twice and cover the pin with half stitch. Weave to the right through one pair on a support pin and put up pin b. Weave to the left through two pairs already in the work and through one pair

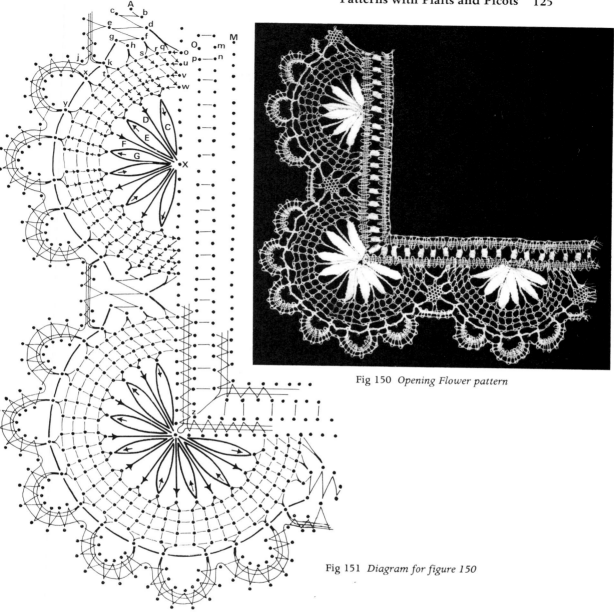

Fig 150 *Opening Flower pattern*

Fig 151 *Diagram for figure 150*

extra from a support pin; put up pin c. Two more pairs are added at d, but only one at e. After e, one pair is left out to become the weaver for the cloth edging and the scallops. After d, f and g, two pairs are left out and the final pin h is covered with half stitch. Plaits are made from d, f, h and g. Three pairs are hung on a support pin behind e and the pair from e travels to the left through two pairs in cloth stitch; the weaver is twisted and then taken through the last pair in cloth stitch and twist. The weaver continues as far as pin j. The two right-hand pairs are plaited to k and work a four-plait crossing with the pairs from g.

Fig. 152 *Pricking for Opening Flower pattern (this pricking is presented here at an angle of 45° clockwise)*

Two pairs are hung on M, the right-hand threads are twisted and the pin covered, then the weaver works through two pairs from a support pin to m. Twist the weaver twice, put up pin m, return to the footside and back to n. Hang one pair on O and weave to the left through two pairs from a support pin and through one pair of the plait from d. Put up pin o and work back through the same passives to p. Use the weaver pairs to make a tally. Leave the tally weaver on the left and work the footside to the next tally. The pair taken in at o is left out at the same pin, and works half stitch, pin q, half stitch with the other plait pair from d. The arrows in the illustration show the direction of the threads; the left-hand pair from q works half stitch, pin r, half stitch with the plait from f. The left-hand pair from r works half stitch, pin s, half stitch with the other pair from the plait from f. Work to pin t.

Return to pin p and weave to the left through the passive pairs and through one pair from q. Put up pin u, and continue the trail.

The second semicircle of ground stitches is worked with pairs from u and r. Continue until the pair from t has been used. After v has been worked, the third semicircle is started. Then, after w has been worked, the final semicircle is worked to release pairs for leaf C and plait D. Work the leaf and plait, and make a crossing at X. Incorporate the weaver as explained for the lace in figure 145 and on page 120. Leave the right-hand pairs and use the left pairs to make leaf E. The pairs travel through the semicircular ground as shown by arrows and come together to plait to x and make a crossing with the pair from k.

A short plait is made to the scallop and the weaver from j works as follows. Check that pin j is covered with cloth stitch and twist and work to the right with the weaver through the plait pairs in cloth stitch. Put up the pin and work back remembering to twist the weaver and make the cloth stitch and twist edge on the left. At the end of the scallop the cloth pairs plait to y, work a crossing and plait for a short distance before separating to travel through the semicircular ground to make plait F. The hanging pair and plait F make a crossing; the same pinhole is used a second time and the left-hand pairs make leaf G. Continue.

In the corner the same method is applied for the scallops, and the arrangement of threads in the footside and trail is shown in the illustration. At z the left-hand pair for the tally is the trail weaver as usual; it makes the tally before the corner is turned. After the corner has been worked the pinhole is used a second time. Notice carefully how the passive pairs and weavers change position and how the passive is used to make the corner tally.

10 – Insertions and Edgings

Six patterns are included here to show a wider use of Torchon stitches. They may be worked in coarse or fine threads, or in a combination within a pattern. The first insertion lends itself very well to a really thick thread and a coarse pattern as an insertion for a bedspread. The second insertion looks equally well if laid over fabric, particularly for dress trimmings. The four wide edgings with corners may be adapted to make insertion matching pieces. When these have been successfully completed, the lacemaker will be well equipped to make original patterns, and not rely on books or fellow enthusiasts for prickings.

HONEYCOMB INSERTION PATTERN

A solid mass of cloth or half stitch creates a strong contrast with the rest of the pattern. These patterns emphasise the value of this as well as giving the lacemaker the opportunity to consider more fully the importance of forethought and preparation before starting the piece of lace. When the pattern is worked out and the design has been transferred to graph paper, or when a pricking has been selected, it is frequently necessary to sketch in the path of the weaver and to work out where each thread will lie. For many designs it is worthwhile making a sample piece of lace. As an example of this, refer to figure 153. The squares of cloth have been worked in three different ways. Only C is balanced; A and B have more cloth at the beginning and fewer rows at the end. In figures 154 and 155 the correct arrangement of cloth threads is shown. The ringed hole at the centre is not used, and a balance is achieved on either side of centre.

The stitch in the centre of the cloth is sometimes known as honeycomb, but it is Torchon honeycomb, and not to be confused with the honeycomb in Bucks Point lace, as the appearance is very different. This arrangement of stitches is often seen in Scandinavian patterns but rarely in English patterns. Figure 156 shows the arrangement of holes on graph paper; referring to this and the photograph, notice the definite diagonal and vertical lines. Figure 153 gives different methods of using the stitches, by placing the holes differently within the given area.

In the first pattern all the pairs from the cloth must be brought in diagonally,

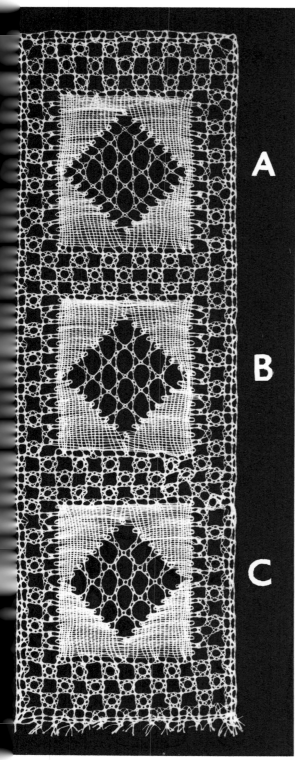

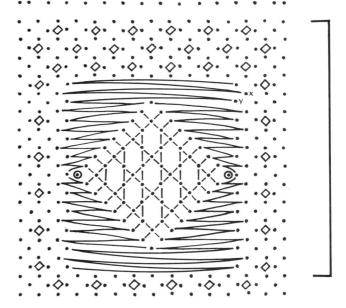

Fig 154 *Diagram for correct cloth stitch arrangement*

53 *Honeycomb Insertion pattern*

otherwise no pairs are available for the diagonal lines near to the cloth. This reduces the vertical lines and changes the pattern. It can be said that this is desirable to emphasise the diamond shape, and that all the oval honeycomb shapes made are complete. Alternatively it can be argued that there should be no distractions within the diamond, and that the pattern within should be perfect. The decision lies with the worker. The holes are arranged differently in the second and third repeats, and the vertical and diagonal lines extend the full distance.

The honeycomb stitch

Refer to figure 153 and the different arrangements of holes for A and B. Figure 154 shows the direction of threads for A and figure 157 for B and C. Referring to photograph 153, it will be seen that the actual method of making the stitches is different in the third repeat from the other two. Both methods are acceptable, and that used in the third repeat seems more attractive. However it is less stable in a Torchon pattern, and unless completely enclosed does not retain its shape.

First method

This method is used in the first and second repeats (153A and B). As the pairs come from cloth, twist them twice each. Make a half stitch before the pin, put up the pin, make a half stitch to cover the pin, and give both pairs one extra twist each. This twist helps to fill the large gaps between the pinholes. As half stitch only is worked before the pin, the pairs continue in the same direction so that a good tension is maintained.

Fig 155 *Detail of C*

Second method

This method is used in the third repeat (153C). As the pairs from cloth enter the work, twist them twice and work half stitch with one twist extra on each pair, then put up the pin and repeat the stitch. The extra twist on the first stitch moves the threads so that there is no continuity. For this reason no reference has been made to a ground stitch, which is occasionally used with this stitch before and after the pin. Unless there is a continuous diagonal thread the tension is poor, and when the article is laundered the lace becomes untidy.

To work the pattern

The pattern is started in the same way as the insertion. The working diagrams, figures 86 and 87, show clearly how the bobbins are introduced. When pairs hang from the top edge they are waiting to be introduced into the rose ground. This has been explained for the pattern on page 76; figure 94 and the accompanying text describe the order of work in detail. Referring to this illustration, it is most important to work pins J, K and L before beginning the units. As threads fall diagonally from the top edge, the choice of pairs is obvious. The same illustration and description shows how the rose ground enters and leaves the cloth stitch.

The weaver for the cloth is marked on figure 154, and it is important to note that the weaver extends to x on one row and only to y on the next, although the cloth is apparently straight at the edge. At x one pair is taken in and discarded; at y there is no pair available, the pin is put up, and the weaver travels back through pairs already in the cloth.

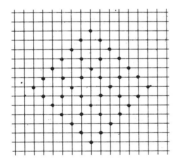

Fig 156 *Arrangement of holes for honeycomb stitch*

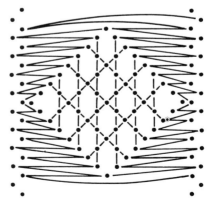

Fig 157 *The direction of threads for B and C*

SPIDER AND ROSE GROUND INSERTION PATTERN

Figure 158 shows another method of using a mass of cloth or half stitch. The diamonds are smaller areas but they still effectively outline the rest of the pattern. Figure 160 explains the working of small triangles near to the footside. These have been worked in half stitch, but they may be worked in cloth stitch if preferred.

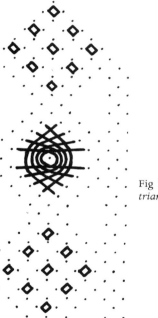

Fig 158 *Spider and Rose Ground Insertion pattern*

Fig 159 *Pricking for Spider and Rose Ground Insertion pattern*

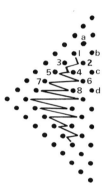

Fig 160 *Working the small triangles near the footside*

A pair from the ground pin a works with a pair coming diagonally from the left in half stitch; pin 1 is put up and covered. The right-hand pair continues to weave through one more pair to pin 2. This pair must have come through from footside pin b. Weave back bringing in a pair on the left. After pin 2, one pair is left out to work the footside and pin c. Meanwhile the triangle is continued and pin 4 put up; nothing enters, nor leaves, at this pin. However at pin 6 a pair is brought in from the footside pin c, and then left out for d. Continue.

Figure 159 gives the pricking with spiders and rose ground, but any other centre may be introduced as an alternative.

TORCHON FEATHER PATTERN

Refer to figures 161 and 162. The only stitches required are cloth and cloth stitch and twist; a cloth stitch and twist ground has been worked to support a very firm pattern. When a definite order of work has been established, the pattern is quick to work.

Fig 161 *Torchon Feather pattern*

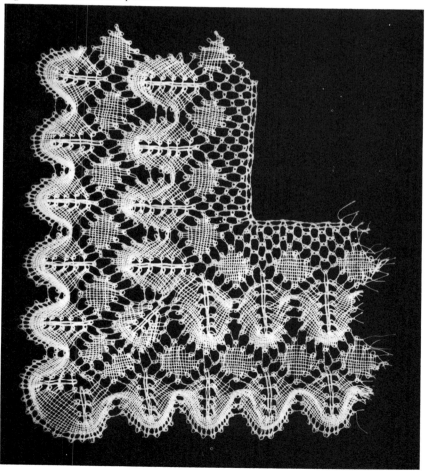

To begin

Work the right-hand diamond and the ground, then work the left-hand diamond.

To work the fan

Hang seven pairs on A, in order, from left to right. The left-hand pair is the weaver and works cloth stitch through the other six pairs on the same pin, and through the next three pairs from the diamond to B. Work the complete fan with a twisted pair on the outside edge, then bring in the fourth pair from the diamond at the base of the fan. Note that pairs are left out on the headside at C and D, and that after C the twisted pair on the headside is temporarily abandoned. Stop at E.

To work the middle fan

Hang three pairs on F in order from left to right. The left-hand pair is the weaver and it works in cloth stitch through the other two pairs and through the next three pairs from the diamond to G. Work the fan, bringing in pairs as indicated in the diagram. From the top centre hole H pairs will be left out as indicated; at pin J nothing is left out, this pin is necessary to achieve an even fan shape. Remember that a similar hole will occur on every repeat, so never leave a pair out at the pin.

The corner

This must be worked to the diagonal line and the pillow turned. Work diamonds K and L, outer fan M, and the middle fan N, as far as pin O. Work diamond P and outer fan Q.

To work the centre small fan

Use the pairs indicated in the illustration to work cloth stitch and twist, then put up pin 1 and cover with cloth stitch and twist. Continue to work pins 2, 3 and 4 using cloth stitch and twist before and after the pin. The right-hand pair at pin 4 becomes the weaver and works the fan using pairs hanging from 3, 2 and 1. Pairs are brought in at q and r. New pairs are joined in at r, s and t for cloth rectangle S. Work to R bringing in one final pair from fan N. When pairs re-enter fan from rectangle V, discard them and knot them neatly. Work the cloth stitch rectangle S and the large corner fan completely, turning the pillow from the centre pin. Begin at T, bring in three pairs from the cloth rectangle and put up pin U. Eventually pin U is used a second time and the pair released to begin rectangle V.

The centre small fan can be worked from R to W. Pins 1, 2 and 3 are worked using cloth stitch and twist before and after the pin. Pin 1 is worked using the weaver from W and the pair to the right of it from the cloth fan. Pin 2 is worked with a pair from pin 1 and another pair from the fan, and pin 3 with the pair from pin 2 and the last cloth pair. Work outer fan X and diamond Y. From pin O work fan Z.

Fig 162 *Diagram for Torchon Feather pattern*

HONEYCOMB AND SPIDER PATTERN

Refer to figures 163 and 164. The instructions for honeycomb are given on page 130. If holes from x to y and z are omitted, the spider D in figure 73 may be substituted. Of course other alterations can be made, but rose ground cannot be used to replace the honeycomb as there is an uneven number of holes within the half stitch.

To begin

Work the ground in preparation for the half stitch trail. Work the half stitch trails, ascertaining from the illustration the direction of the weaver in each trail. In this pattern the trails must match each other. Half stitch ground is worked from x to y before the spider is made, the spider is described on page 62.

To work the fan

Before working the fan, pairs are introduced from the right and the row of ground stitches worked from y to z; the pins from q to r are also completed. The weaver for the fan has no pin on the edge. In order to support the weaver to begin, it is necessary to make a hole at s, put up a pin and hang a weaver up to work with the pair from q in cloth stitch and twist. Continue to the right in cloth stitch and work the fan as in the illustration. At position S the weaver completes the fan and lies on the outside edge. When the ground stitches which surround the spider have been worked, the weaver at S will begin the next fan. It is important to obliterate the hole added at s as it may cause confusion when the pattern is re-used.

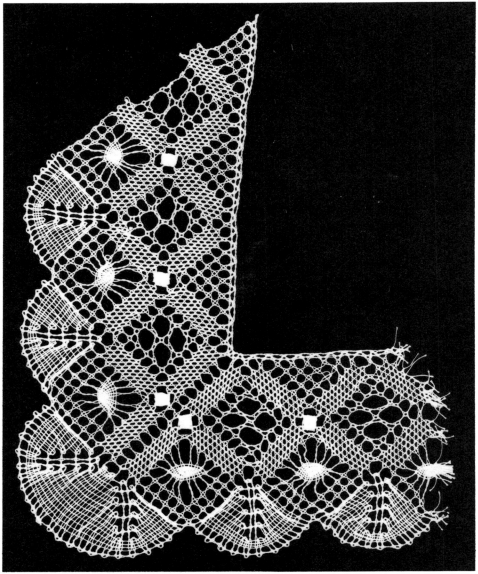

Fig 163 *Honeycomb and Spider pattern*

The tally
Never make the tally until it is required, otherwise it will lose its shape.

The corner
The corner is straightforward, work to the diagonal, work the corner pin, turn the pillow and continue.

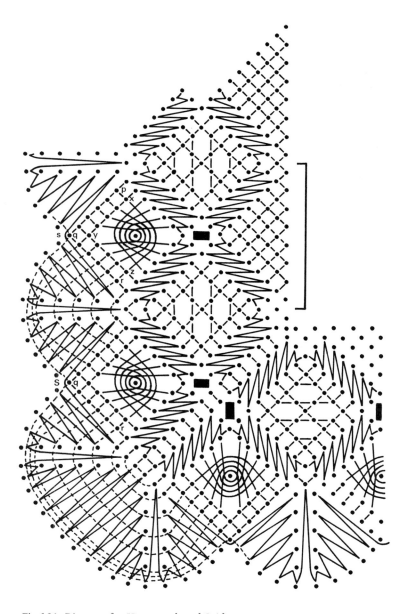

Fig 164 *Diagram for Honeycomb and Spider pattern*

ROSE GROUND AND DAISY PATTERN

Refer to figures 165 and 166. This pattern shows an unusual but very attractive way of working leaves out of rose ground. The half stitch in the trail and in the small triangles emphasise the 'trail' of rose ground. The fan weaver uses a heavier thread; compare it with the fan in figure 167.

Fig 165 *Rose Ground and Daisy pattern*

To begin

There are two twisted passive pairs in the footside as in figure 148. Work the half stitch triangle. The half stitch trail is started at A with a weaver on pin A. Seven pairs are hung on a support pin behind. Work the trail joining in one new pair at every pin on the left, and leaving out at every pin on the right. Remember to work pins B and C in the same way as in the pattern on page 36.

Fig 166 *Diagram for Rose Ground and Daisy pattern*

The rose ground

To begin the rose ground hang two pairs on a support pin to the left of D and two pairs on another support pin to the right of D. Work the rose ground unit. Continue to work the rose ground units alongside the trail and the triangle as far as possible.

The cloth work

In the cloth work, note that the pinholes are close together at E. This is necessary to achieve a symmetrical result.

The fan

The fan has been worked using pearl cotton no. 12 and the rest of the pattern in Fils à Dentelles no. 70 (DMC threads). The heavier thread launders more easily and lies flat when the lace is in use. The pearl cotton is not highly twisted and it works an even fan very readily.

The spider

When the fan has been worked to a, the weaver is well twisted as it works to the spider. The spider has three pairs from the trail on the right and the two pairs from the fan on the left. The weaver is the third pair on the left.

The daisy

For the daisy within the rose ground framework, check that all the rose ground units are completed with the final cloth stitch and twist. Work rows of the half stitch, pin, half stitch ground from F to G and F to H. Pairs from adjacent pinholes work half stitch, pin, half stitch to begin each leaf. Work six leaves.

To work the centre of the daisy, take the right-hand pair from the top left-hand leaf and the left-hand pair from the top right-hand leaf and work half stitch. Put up the first pin. The pair to the left of the pin becomes the weaver and works, in half stitch, to the right through the next three pairs. Put up the pin and the second leaf is part of the half stitch centre. Work to the left and bring in the next leaf. Continue bringing in and leaving out at the points of the diamond, complete the diamond and work six more leaves. Finish each leaf with a half stitch, put up the pin at the end of the leaf and cover with half stitch. Work from G to J and H to J. Complete the rose ground units.

The corner

The corner is worked to the diagonal line and the pillow turned. Work to pin K (ie work half the spider and put up pin K). Take the fan weaver back out to the left and continue the fan until K is reached the second time. Work through the two pairs to the left of pin K with the fan weaver, remove pin K and replace to the left of the weaver. Complete the spider and the fan.

ROSE GROUND AND HALF STITCH BORDER PATTERN

Refer to figures 167 and 168 which give an interesting combination of these two stitches, also the pattern includes yet another variation of the Torchon fan.

To begin

Three rows of ground are worked in preparation for the half stitch trail. Put up pin at A and hang up the weaver for the trail. Work to the right through two pairs from a support pin and through one pair from the ground, put up pin B and continue to b. Another trail is started with a weaver on a pin at C. This works to the right through three pairs on a support pin to pin D; continue with this trail to the fan.

Fig 167 *Rose Ground and Half Stitch Border pattern*

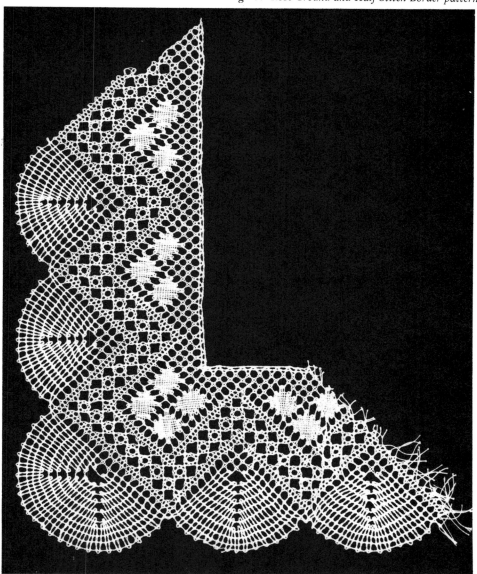

The rose ground

To begin the rose ground unit at E, two pairs are hung on a support pin to the left and two pairs from the trail used on the right. A very definite stitch is required within the half stitch trails, and rose ground in figure 60A has been selected for the example shown.

Fig 168 *Diagram for Rose Ground and Half Stitch Border pattern*

The fan

At pin F, hang two pairs on the pin. Twist twice, and work the right hand two threads to G. The left-hand threads become the fan weaver, work the fan according to the illustration to J, but do not put up the pin. Remember that it will be necessary to work pin o before the weaver can travel to J. Pins p and H are worked, and the left-hand pair from H works out to J. This will match the work from F to G. At J the weaver and the pair from H work together in cloth stitch and twist, pin J is put up and covered with cloth stitch and twist.

The corner

Work to the corner diagonal line. The half stitch trails finish at b and d, and pairs are left out at a and c. It will be seen in the photograph that there is a definite break in the outer trail but the inner is apparently continuous.

The inner trail

Complete the half stitch and cover pin b. The pair from a and the right hand pair from b work one half stitch.

The outer trail

Complete the trail to d and cover the pin. No extra stitches are worked. Either the inner or the outer trail method is acceptable, but the same should be used in both trails.

Grids

A   1mm. Useful for identifying distance apart of holes on prickings and lace. Too fine for normal work.

B   1.5mm ($\frac{1}{16}$'').

C   2mm ($\frac{1}{12}$'').

D   2.5mm ($\frac{1}{10}$'').

E   3mm ($\frac{1}{8}$'').

F   5mm ($\frac{1}{5}$'') Useful for working out a pattern to be reduced for use.

G   Polar graph used for making grids as explained on page

H   Polar graph.

I   Square grid. Little used, refer to page 102.

J   Normal arrangement of holes.

K   Enlargement of J.

L   Grid with tallies on the footside.

M   Grid suitable for a wide pattern, there is a break in the centre.

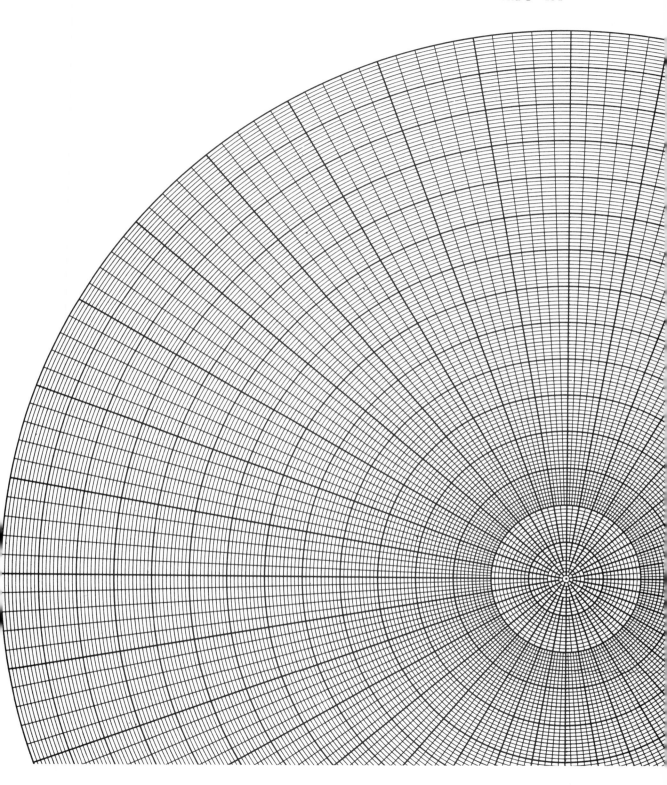

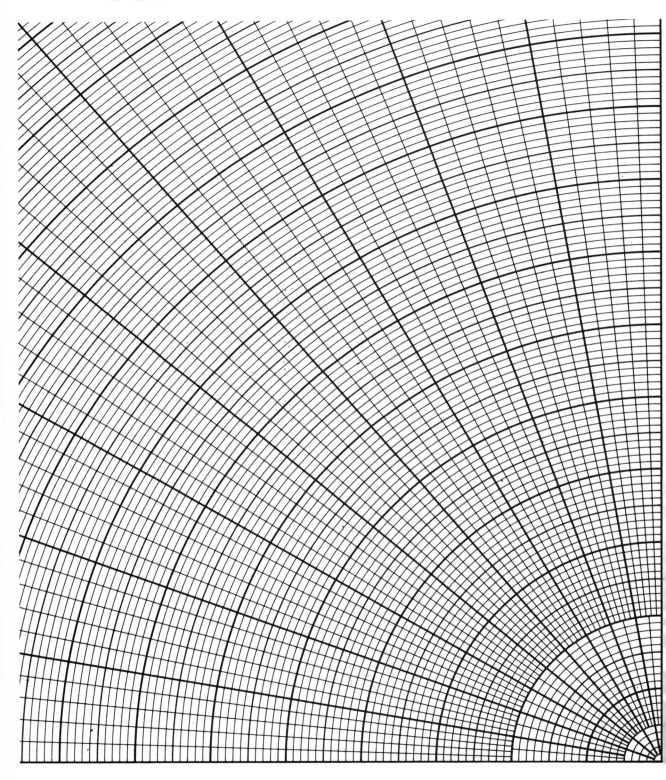

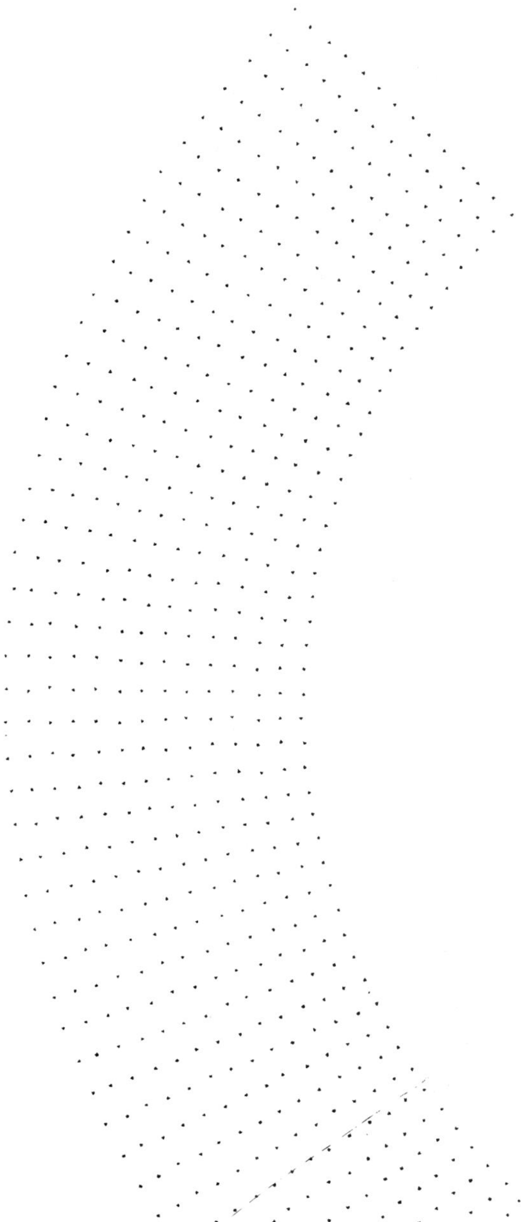

Grid J

Grid K

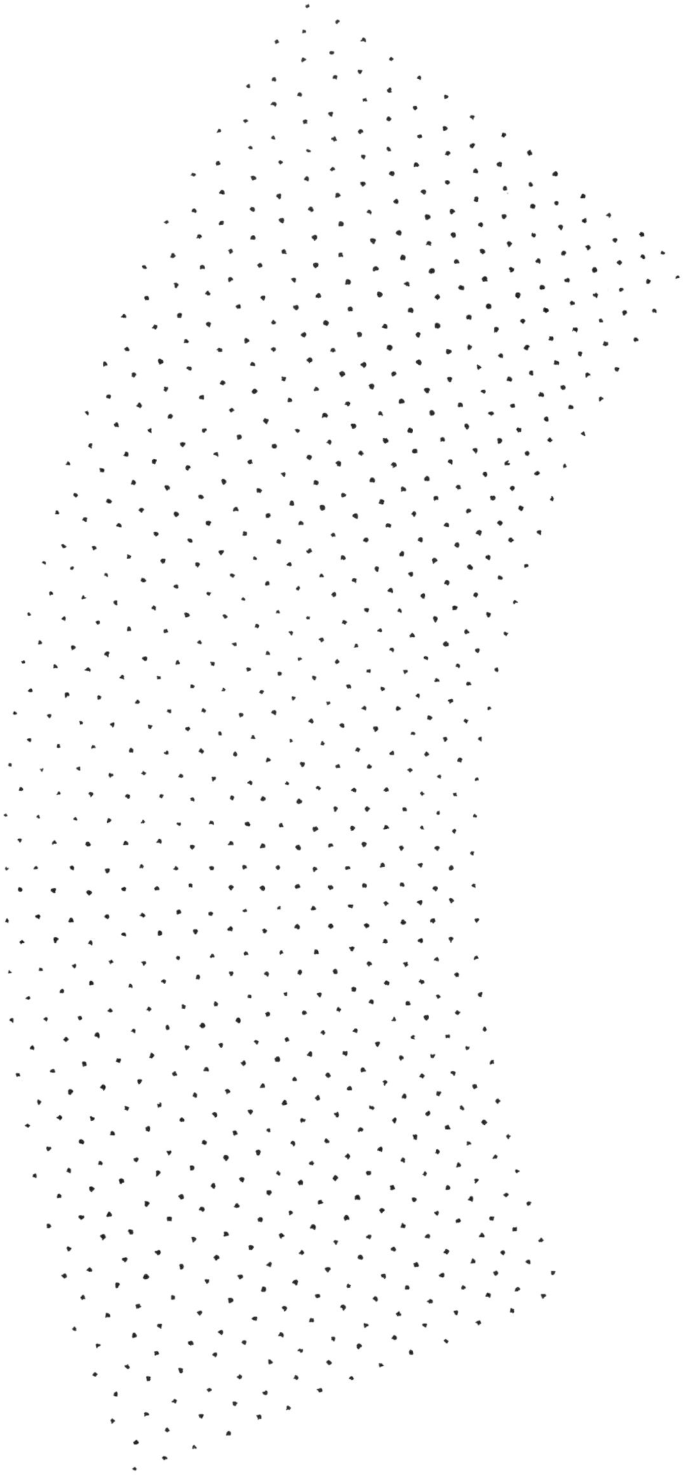

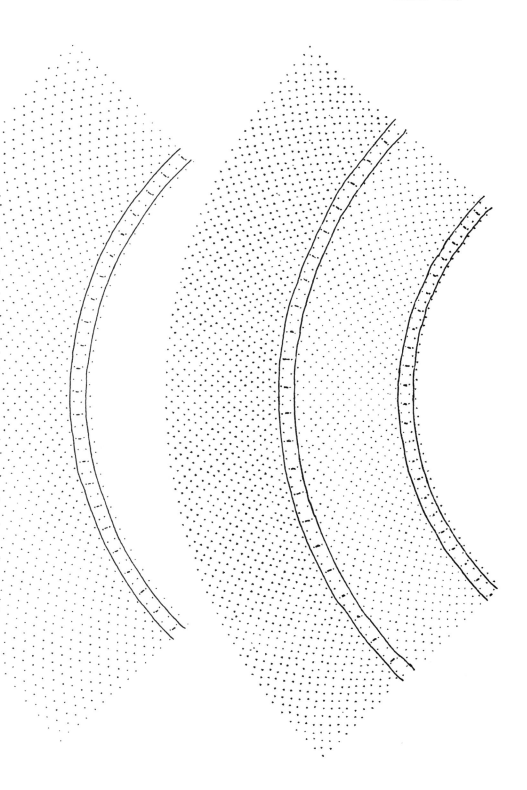

Suppliers

UK

Audrey Sells
49 Pedley Lane
Clifton
Shefford
Bedfordshire
All lace making requisites (mail order service)

D.J. Hornsby (woodturner)
149 High Street
Burton Latimer
Kettering
Northants
All lacemaking requisites; plain, ornamental and inscribed bobbins in wood and bone; pillow stands; bobbin winders; turned picture frames and trays with glass or PVC fronts (mail order service).

The Needlewoman Shop
146 Regent Street
London W1
Lace threads, pins and bobbins (mail order service)

E. Braggins & Sons
26–36 Silver Street
Bedford
Bedfordshire
Lacemaking equipment, materials and books

Mace & Nairn
89 Crane Street
Salisbury
Wiltshire SP1 2PY
Lacemaking equipment, materials and books

USA

Berga-Ullman, Inc.
P.O. Box 918
North Adams, Massachusetts 01247
Materials and equipment

Frederick J. Fawcett
129 South Street
Boston, Massachusetts 02130
Large selection of linen yarns and threads

Osma G. Tod Studio
319 Mendoza Avenue
Coral Gables, Florida 33134
Books, instructions, materials and equipment

Robin and Russ Handweavers
533 N. Adams Street
McMinnville, Oregon 97128
Books, materials and equipment

Some Place
2990 Adeline Street
Berkeley, California 94703
Books, instructions, materials and equipment

The Unique and Art Lace Cleaners
5926 Delmar Boulevard
St. Louis, Missouri 63112
Professional lace cleaning and restoration

Bibliography

Channer, C.C., *Lacemaking, Bucks Point Ground*, Dryad Press

Devonia, *The Honiton Lace Book*, Paul Minet, 1972

Freeman, Charles, *Pillow Lace in the East Midlands,* Borough of Luton Museum and Art Gallery

Hopewell, *Bobbin and Pillow Lace*, Shire Publications

Luxton, Elsie, *The Technique of Honiton Lace,* Batsford, London; Charles T. Branford Co, USA, 1979

Maidment, Margaret, *A Manual of Handmade Bobbin Lace*, Paul Minet

Martin, Peggy, *Bobbin Lace: Step by Step Basic*, P. Martin

Nottingham, Pamela, *The Technique of Bobbin Lace,* Batsford, London; Van Nostrand Reinhold, USA, 1976

Olsson, Inga-Lisa, *Knypplerskan I, II, III*, Forlag A/BE Homqvists EFTR, Malmo, Sweden (with supplement in English)

Wright, Thomas, *The Romance of the Lace Pillow*, Paul Minet

Index